# THE
# CLEVELAND SPORTS
# LEGACY
# SINCE 1945

# THE
# CLEVELAND SPORTS
# LEGACY
# SINCE 1945

## Edited by Mark Hodermarsky

## CLEVELAND LANDMARKS PRESS
### Cleveland

# PUBLISHING INFORMATION

LIBRARY OF CONGRESS CATALOG CARD NUMBER: 91-077472

ISBN: 0-936760-06-0

PUBLISHED BY

CLEVELAND LANDMARKS PRESS, INC.

13610 SHAKER BOULEVARD #503

CLEVELAND, OHIO  44120-1592

PRINTED BY

BROWN  BUSINESS GRAPHICS, INC.

CLEVELAND, OHIO

# DEDICATION

To the memory of my father, George Hodermarsky, who always found time to play catch with me.

To my mother, Elizabeth, who always supported my interest in sports.

To Lynda, whose love sustains me.

# ACKNOWLEDGEMENTS

Special thanks to the following for their help and guidance: Cuyahoga County Library (Fairview Regional Branch), Cleveland Public Library, Cleveland State University, Cleveland Indians, Cleveland Browns, The Pro Football Hall of Fame, St. Ignatius High School, James Toman, Ed Nolan, Bob Ward, Bill Becker, Milton Turner, Dan Rourke, Joe Toner, Art Thomas, Pierre Davignon, Mike Hodermarsky, and Roger Perry.

# CONTENTS

# INTRODUCTION

Cleveland—a town of historic firsts in modern sports history. Larry Doby became the first black American League ballplayer in 1947. A year later Satchel Paige arrived to become the first black in the majors to win a game and to pitch a shutout (both in his first major-league start). In that dramatic 1948 season, Satch also became the first black to pitch in a World Series game. And in 1975 Frank Robinson became the game's first black manager.

Cleveland—where many of the greatest sports legends displayed their extraordinary athletic gifts: Bob Feller, Otto Graham, and Jim Brown. In addition to these three sporting giants, who arguably were the best to have ever played at their respective positions, Cleveland boasts a lengthy list of other hall of famers in baseball, football and basketball.

Cleveland—a city which has seen its share of potentially fabled stars struck down by either death (Ernie Davis and Don Rogers) or by serious injury (Herb Score).

Cleveland—where fans enjoyed a decade of unsurpassed glory by their professional teams. After the Cleveland Rams won the NFL Championship in 1945, the Browns (led by quarterback Otto Graham and coaching genius Paul Brown) appeared in ten consecutive championship games, winning seven. The Indians won it all, of course, in 1948, and in 1954 won more games (111) than any team in American League history. During those other years, the Tribe would fall just short of the powerful Yankees. Between 1946 and 1955 the Barons, of the American Hockey League, won four Calder Cups.

Cleveland—where fans have suffered in anguish on more than a few occasions. The trades of Rocky Colavito and Paul Warfield, Red Right 88, The Drive, and The Fumble are among the more disheartening events. Certainly the most unendurable episode has been witnessing the ineptitude of the

Indians for the last 32 years.

Even during some of the lean years, the decade of the seventies, for instance, great moments awakened the attention of Cleveland's fans—Chris Chambliss won rookie-of-the-year honors; Gaylord Perry took the Cy Young Award; Dick Bosman and Dennis Eckersley tossed no-hitters. In football the Browns came within seconds of ruining the unblemished record of the heralded 1972 Miami Dolphins in an exciting playoff contest. The Cavaliers enjoyed their most thrilling season in their history during this decade with the "Miracle in Richfield."

This city supports its sports teams in record numbers. Cleveland owns most of the attendance records in both football and baseball; the Barons and Cavs have also drawn record throngs; major golf tournaments attract sizable crowds. And these knowledgeable fans cheer as loudly as any group of sports disciples anywhere.

These avid followers of sport also have turned enthusiastically to the local sports pages, to some of the finest columnists and beat writers in the country, to better understand and savor these unforgettable moments in Cleveland sports history. Franklin "Whitey" Lewis, Frank Gibbons, Bob August and Bob Sudyk of the *Cleveland Press* and Gordon Cobbledick, James E. Doyle, Chuck Heaton, Russell Schneider, Hal Lebovitz and Bill Livingston of the *Plain Dealer* are among some of the scribes who have helped Cleveland's readers to relive these momentous events. Doug Clarke of the *Cleveland Edition*, Terry Pluto of the *Beacon Journal* and A. S. "Doc" Young of the *Call and Post* have provided, along with their peers, insightful reflections on notable Cleveland sporting occurrences and/or Cleveland's professional athletes.

The following pages, then, illuminate, by means of most of the aforementioned writers and some others, many of the most unforgettable moments in Cleveland sports history. Their voices have preserved a legacy—the Cleveland sports legacy.

# Rams Edge 'Skins in Bitter Cold

by JOHN DIETRICH

12/45

The winners and champions of all the football universe—Adam Walsh and his band of valiant Cleveland Rams.

In a triumphant and dramatic finish to the long, stubborn quest that began way back in 1937, a Cleveland team that ranks with the greatest of all time yesterday vanquished the famed Washington Redskins, 15 to 14, for the National League championship and the undisputed world title.

By a margin of one point, in a game of history played in actual zero weather before 32,178 fans in Cleveland Stadium, the Rams ended eight seasons of gloomy adversity to reach the end of the rainbow.

Luck was with them—and they deserved it.

Jim Gillette of Virginia raced in the van, dashing over a slippery gridiron spotted with ice and snow, for a total of 101 yards.

Bob Waterfield, from sun-kissed California, connected 14 of his brilliant forward passes through the zero gale lashing in off Lake Erie.

Big Jim Benton from Arkansas and Gillette hauled down the soaring football with freezing hands, and sped goalward for two touchdowns.

And all the while a tremendous Ram line, hammering away under bitter weather conditions unequaled in football records, was holding the shattering Washington power attack to just 32 yards in 60 minutes.

A game for history—and fortune at last smiled on the Rams, where it had frowned so many times before.

An unprecedented weird play for an automatic safety, in which a daring pass by Sammy Baugh from behind the

1

Mr. and Mrs. Bob Waterfield (Jane Russell)

Washington goal line struck the goal posts and bounced back into the end zone, gave the Rams a two-point lead after nine minutes of play in the first quarter.

It was a break that could happen only in pro football, where the goal posts are on the goal line rather than at the back of the end zone, as in the college game.

The Redskins took the lead, 7-2, at 5:31 of the second period on a 38-yard touchdown forward pass play from Frank Filchock to flying Steve Bagarus of Notre Dame. Joe Aguirre made the conversion.

Then, in the 12th minute of the second quarter, the Rams surged in front as Benton grabbed a Waterfield pass and raced for a touchdown, a gain of 37 yards.

That brought the Rams' second big break of this crucial struggle that settled world gridiron supremacy for 1945.

On Waterfield's place kick for the extra point the ball was partially blocked and knocked high enough that it just crossed the bar. The ball struck the bar, teetered an instant and then dropped over—into the end zone. A wabble the other way and the game would have ended in a tie.

For Gillette, the fast right halfback whose prowess scarcely is recognized outside Cleveland, it was the game of all time.

Opening the second half, the Rams marched 81 yards for the second touchdown. Gillette galloped off tackle and around the ends to lead the advance beyond the mid-field.

With the ball on the Washington 44, Gillette darted down the center, made a brilliant catch of Waterfield's pass, over his shoulder, and galloped nine yards for the score. Waterfield's try for the point was wide, and the score was 15 to 7.

Washington scored again in the final minute of the third period. A 50-yard pass play, Filchock to the flashing Bagarus, put the ball on the Cleveland 6.

Tackle Gil Bouley then threw Filchock for an 11-yard loss, but the Redskins had the ball back on the Cleveland 9, with fourth down coming up.

There the Rams were hoodwinked as never before this season. On fourth down, halfback Bob Seymour whisked away over the goal line, near the sideline and without a Ram within 20 yards, caught a touchdown pass from Filchock. Aguirre, the former St. Mary's end, kicked the point to make it 15-14.

And so this classic struggle eventually ended, with Cleveland one point ahead, but the game was far from won.

Twice in the tense final quarter, the usually deadly Aguirre attempted field goals, either one of which would have wiped out the Rams' slim lead.

On his first, with the ball set up on Cleveland's 31, the kick was wide of the uprights. The second was 10 yards further out and this one fizzled badly.

It was Albie Reisz, second string quarterback from Lorain, who yesterday appeared as a capable running halfback, who clamped down the lid for keeps on Washington's hopes.

In the final minute, Filchock threw a pass from deep in his own territory. Reisz intercepted and ran back 16 yards to the Washington 29. Waterfield was holding the ball and banging into the line as the game ended.

It was a triumph not only for the Rams, who never until this season had cut any figure in the National League race, but also for professional football. When more than 32,000 fans, bundled in blankets, galoshes, and ear muffs, will struggle through zero weather to see a football game, there is no longer any question. The pros have arrived to stay.

For all that this was the worst weather ever encountered in the 13 National League playoffs since 1933, the game was a huge financial success. The gross gate of $164,542, the players' pool of $95,261, and the individual split for the players, set new league records.

Each Ram received $1,469.74 for this one day's work well done, which is $20 more per man than that won by the winning New York Giants last season.

In any kind of reasonable weather conditions, this game would have packed the stadium with 80,000 fans—but that's another story.

The pot of gold was there at the end of the rainbow, as it should be.

# Wounded Veteran Wins U. S. Open in Second Playoff Round

## by JACK CLOWSER

### 6/46

If ever a man deserved the maximum financial return that gilds the path of the United States Open golf champion, he is Lloyd Mangrum, ex-Army corporal, wounded hero of the European combat, and possessor of a magic wand on the putting green.

In a stupendous, eye-popping finish amid the lash of rain, howling wind and crashing thunder, 31-year-old, 145-pound Mangrum won the greatest of all golf crowns yesterday at Canterbury. Seldom, in the history of the sport, has there been an exhibition so fraught with drama as the double playoff staged by Mangrum, Byron Nelson, and Vic Ghezzi.

Mangrum won by shooting a par round, 72, in the afternoon, while the other two carded 73's. All had tied with 72's in the first playoff during the morning.

Mangrum will be a popular champion. He took a terrific beating in the war, and deserves the best of everything. For six months he lay in a French hospital after a jeep accident had shattered his left arm and shoulder so severely that he wondered whether his golf swing would survive. They moulded a cast around his arm and back while a broken humerus and scapula healed.

That wasn't all. While fighting with the 90th Infantry, a German sniper shot him in the right knee, and a piece of shrapnel creased his chin. It's a fine chin, though, and Mangrum has it up, knowing that the game he loves is finally going to pay big dividends for him.

Lloyd Mangrum, 1946 U. S. Open Champion, and his magic putter

Here's the kind of fellow Mangrum is. Hardly had he won the championship than, in a press interview in the steaming locker room, he was assuring us all that "Nelson's the best player we have—he can hit as accurately with a driver as the rest of us can with a mashie-niblick."

Here's the story of Mangrum's triumph in a nutshell. The regulation number of putts for 18 holes of golf is 36. Lloyd used exactly 23 putts on that final round. You simply can't lick that kind of putting. Ghezzi was playing as well as he ever played in his life, especially around the greens, but he couldn't match that, although he only had 29 putts himself. Nelson, from tee to green, was masterful as usual.

But, in the last 36 holes, he could get down only one lengthy putt, a 14-footer.

Nelson held the lead for only one hole in the morning round. He rolled in a downhill 9-foot putt on the second green for a birdie three. On the third hole, 176 yards, he lost the advantage when Ghezzi knocked in a 35-foot putt, Mangrum following suit by making his 20-footer. Nelson's tee shot had stopped only seven feet from the cup, but it must have looked twice that length to him after his adversaries had putted. He missed it, and that was to be the story of a good many greens afterward—Nelson knocking the ball up inside them, then watching their great putting put him under almost unbearable tension.

For the morning 18, Nelson shot 36-36—72, the other two, 34-38—72. From the 13th hole on through the 17th, Byron made up a stroke on either one of the other players until they were all square going to the 18th tee. This was a "sudden death" hole for anyone who faltered, but all carded pars. It was almost a miracle comeback for Nelson, who had been four strokes behind Mangrum after the latter's poor approach at the 12th had hopped over a big trap and curled in close to the pin. He got a birdie on it.

Starting the afternoon 18, Mangrum chipped into the cup at the first hole—after his approach, headed well past the green, had hit a spectator and stopped dead.

Nelson and Ghezzi played sparkling 34's on that nine.  On the ninth hole, 567 yards, Mangrum hooked his drive out of bounds and incurred a stroke and distance penalty.  Shaken, he hit a low slice into the rough, and seemed headed for disaster.  He swatted a long wood shot from that spot, followed by an iron almost 40 feet to the side of the flag, and then stroked the tremendous putt into the hole for a bogey six and a 36.

Nelson lost a stroke in a trap below the 11th green, and Ghezzi took temporary command.  On the 13th, however, the hole where the gallery practically pushed Nelson's caddie into the ball the preceding day and cost him from winning the title outright, Byron came to grief again.  His second was pushed to the right of the green, and he was stymied by a tree.  Forced to play out for the back of the green, he three-putted from 28 feet, missing a two-footer.

Mangrum hit a beautiful pitch shot on the hole, and stopped it close to the flag for a birdie four.  Lloyd really put the clincher on at the 15th and 16th, however.  He waved his wand and it was good for a birdie with a 15-footer on the 15th.  Then, as the storm broke and it became so dark the flight of balls could not be followed, he hit another great pitch shot on the long 16th, and got a six-footer for a birdie that put him two under par and two stokes under both Nelson and Ghezzi.

Nelson's last chance went at the 230-yard 17th, where he drove 18 feet over the green and his ball came to rest where he had to cut through a tuft of grass and earth before his club could touch the ball.  He dribbled it to the edge of the green, and took a bogey four.  Mangrum missed the green, pitched on and also got a four, to Ghezzi's three.

On the last hole, 441 yards, uphill, Mangrum  hit his second into a trap short of the green, while Ghezzi was just over but on the short-clipped surface, and Nelson was on the front edge.  Mangrum exploded out short, and had to get that one down to win,  provided Ghezzi didn't sink the five-footer he left himself after he chipped on.  Big Vic's putt stopped a half-inch short of the hole, and away flew his chance.  Nelson went down in the regulation two for par, but that didn't matter.

Everything hung on Mangrum's five-foot putt.

The battle-scarred war veteran, his thin shoulders drooping and rain-soaked, called once more for the magic wand. Over the rain-soaked surface, the ball ran straight into the cup. Lloyd Mangrum, born a farm boy, and a caddie from the time he could tote a bag, was Open golf champion of the United States.

Ghezzi took it hard, and could scarcely be consoled in the locker room. He didn't go to the radio tent for the coast-to-coast broadcast, but Nelson did, and when following Mangrum on the air, laughed good-naturedly as they handed him the mike.

"Just give me one of those Gillette blades you're plugging, and I'll cut my throat," he cracked.

Tribe fans celebrate.

# Doby and Paige Help Tribe Win

# Pennant

## by A. S. "DOC" YOUNG
## 10/48

"Whe-e-e-e-e" went the whistles, "ding-dong" went the bells, "clap-clap-clap" went 2,000,000 hands as the the Cleveland Indians won their first pennant since 1920 when they beat the Boston Red Sox 8 to 3 in the first American League play-off at Boston's Fenway Park on Monday. The play-off was made necessary on Sunday when the Indians were beaten 7 to 1 by Hal Newhouser and the Detroit Tigers while the Boston Red Sox were pasting a 10 to 5 loss on the New York Yankees.

It was a fitting finish to the most hectic season in baseball history and the reward for the never-say-die efforts of a fighting bunch of ball players who, during their pennant chase, had experienced many moments of awkwardness, long hours of despair, a season chock full of crucial games, but who licked them all to win the gol-durndest league race by one full game.

The Indians were relegated to fourth place by most of the "experts" who cared enough to make a prediction. But a series of unexpected developments altered that dismal picture into the rosy portrait of a championship club. It was a season which saw the Indians break fast and, except for a few days, lead the league right down the stretch. Then, the Indians faded and were all but counted out as Joe McCarthy's ball-massaging Red Sox made their play and the New York Yankees edged into first place for a few hilarious hours.

But the Indians fought back and while the Red Sox and the Yankees were being kayoed on their last Western trip and while they were knocking each other around in the East, the Tribe pushed its way back into the lead. As late as last Thursday, the prospect of a Cleveland pennant was pretty clear, but with a two-game lead and three games with Detroit, Cleveland blew the lead. The Tigers took two out of three and a play-off was required to settle the issue.

You know what happened: Lou Boudreau unlimbered his bat, Doby did likewise, and Gene Bearden flexed the arm which had only one day's rest, and when the batting, hitting, running, and throwing were over, it was a championship for the Tribe!

A few paragraphs back we wrote of unexpected developments which changed the Tribe's pennant picture. Two of the most important were Larry Doby's totally unexpected hitting and fielding and Satchel Paige's pitching help that came in the dog days of the race.

Larry grew into a major league center fielder with no previous experience at the spot. He finished the season with an even .300 batting average. In the last month of play, Doby led all the Indians at bat with a near .400 average. His big bat won important games along the way and his fielding, with few exceptions, was steady—sometimes brilliant.

Doby concluded the regular season with 130 hits in 433 times at bat. His hits went for 211 total bases, including 21 doubles, 9 triples, and 14 home runs. Larry scored 82 runs and batted in 65 tallies. He walked 54 times, stole nine bases, and struck out 75 times. He was the third highest batter of Indians who played 100 or more games.

Paige's play was spectacular and it was his presence that contributed many thousands to the attendance record, enabling the Indians to draw 2,620,527 fans for a major league season's record. On the mound, despite his age (40-44), Satch was well-night amazing: He led the Indians' pitchers in earned run average with an unofficial mark of 2.50. Bob Lemon, the big winner who posted 10 shutouts, had an earned run average of 2.79 and Gene Bearden, the freshman left hander, posted a 2.54 for regular season play. These averages do not include fractional innings pitched.

Toward the end of the season, however, Paige was not used.

Lou Boudreau, the manager, told the writer that Satch was not in the doghouse. But rumors persist that Satch had fallen out of Lou's good graces and it certainly looked that way last Sunday when the manager called in two rookie pitchers while Paige was ignored completely. But if Boudreau's words are to be taken for the truth, then Satch deserved to have had a hand in the final games.

Paige led the Indians in won-lost average with six games won and only one defeat for an average of .857. He appeared in 21 games, pitched 72 2/3 innings, allowed 61 hits, 20 earned runs, 22 bases on balls, struck out 43, pitched three complete games, and was reached for only two homers by opposing batters.

The signing of Paige was a bold stroke for President Bill Veeck. It was the final clincher at the gate and Paige came through to help the Indians when the pitching forces seemed about ready to falter completely.

The Indians' feat was the more amazing when it is considered that for most of the season the outfield was unsettled. It wasn't until the second home stand that Doby became a regular—and he promptly sprained his ankle after hitting .412 for the stand. After Satch came, the pitching became more settled, with Lemon, Bearden, and the rejuvenated Feller contributing important wins.

Lou Boudreau, despite his injuries played a magnificent game at short and with the willow, aging Ken Keltner experienced his best season, and Joe Gordon, the former Yankee, returned to his great form.

It was a great season and a great many stars had a hand in the victory. But, there's no forgetting the contribution of Larry Doby and Satchel Paige . . . for they helped a lot!

The 1948 World Champions

# Baseball's World Champions

## by FRANKLIN "WHITEY" LEWIS
## 10/48

Not since the heyday of the great Yankee teams had an American League entry been such a favorite going into a World Series as were Boudreau's battle-weary Indians. Whatever leanings even the staunchest followers of the Braves had toward the National League representative were obliterated in Brooklyn four days before the close of the championship season.

The Braves had clinched the pennant, mainly on the stout pitching of Johnny Sain, the aggressive play of a rookie shortstop, Alvin Dark, the timely batting of Tommy Holmes, and the slugging of the one-time Tribe problem child, Jeff Heath, and of Bob Elliot. But Heath, sliding into the plate at Ebbets Field, had caught his spikes and fractured an ankle. The Braves' stock against whichever team won the American League's torrid race went down kerplunk.

The Indians were tired, to be sure, but they were still moving speedily on the momentum supplied by the wild finish of their own campaign. Then, too, a rundown of their pitching and batting achievements made them all the more formidable.

Boudreau batted .355 to finish second to Ted Williams in the individual race. Mitchell compiled a fancy .366 average, while the rookie Doby, only a year and a half out of semipro ranks, surged over the .300 mark in the last few days to wind up with .301. Keltner just missed the charmed circle with .297.

The Tribe had power to burn. Gordon batted in 124 runs and added 32 home runs. Keltner drove in 119 and hit 31 circuit smashes. Boudreau batted in 106 runs and contributed 18 homers. Robinson had 16 home runs and 83 runs batted in. The regular infielders batted across 432 runs! Allie Clark, scourge of left-handed pitchers, stroked .310. Jim Hegan batted only .248 but caught 144 games and was far and away the best all-around backstop in his league.

There were two twenty-game pitchers, Bearden and Lemon. The great Feller had been stopped at nineteen, but he came through at the right times. The Braves had no three pitchers to match the Cleveland trio.

"Power will win for the Indians," ran almost every prediction on the World Series.

Yet seldom has there been a World Series with less power revealed or with less animation by the players. The Indians were tired at the outset. After their triumph in the league race, anything else must be anticlimactic.

The tone of the Series was established in the first game when Feller tangled with Sain, the Braves' twenty-four-game star. They dueled in brilliance through seven innings. Feller did not allow a hit until the fifth and not another until the eighth. Sain gave up singles to Doby, Gordon, Keltner, and Hegan.

Neither team had had a runner as far as third base in the seven innings. Feller wavered at the start of the eighth and walked Bill Salkeld. Phil Masi ran for his fellow catcher. Mike McCormick's sacrifice moved Masi to second. Eddie Stanky was passed intentionally.

The stage was set for the most controversial play of the Series and one that will be discussed for generations. Ever since Boudreau had managed the Indians, he and Feller had collaborated on a pick-off play at second base. The throw is based on the count by the pitcher and the fielder that is started on a prearranged signal. The best base runners in the business had been trapped off second and retired on Bob's precisely timed throws.

Masi wandered off the cushion. Boudreau sneaked behind him and dashed for second. Feller wheeled and threw. Masi, startled, flung himself headlong at the bag. Boudreau tagged him on the shoulder.

Bill Stewart of the National League, umpiring at second

base, flattened his palms over the ground. "Safe," he ruled. Boudreau charged him, yelling and objecting. Feller and Gordon joined in the complaining. The jockeys on the Cleveland bench went to work on Stewart. But Masi remained safe, naturally.

Feller retired Sain, but Holmes slapped a sizzling ground single into left, and Masi raced over the plate with the only run of the game. Feller's two-hit masterpiece had been wasted, and 40,135 Bostonians went away in high glee.

Lemon squared the Series the next day with a 4-to-1 victory before 39,633. Bob bobbed and weaved a little in the first inning but settled down to scatter the Braves' remaining six hits one to an inning. Manager Billy Southworth of the Braves nominated his ace southpaw, Warren Spahn, but the Redskins ran him off the hill in the fifth. Boudreau and Doby, each with a double and single, were the big guns in the Cleveland attack. A sensational double play by Boudreau and Gordon lifted the game above the routine.

In the first two games, no murderous clouting had been registered. But those who had predicted that the Tribe's power would decide the Series took new hope as the teams entrained for Cleveland and the next three games. The players of both teams were overjoyed in their pocketbooks. No matter how the Series ended, their individual shares of receipts would be close to record size.

There were many ticket snafus before the opener in Cleveland's sprawling stadium, and instead of a jam-packed park, the third game was started before only 70,306 customers. Rested three days since his sensational victory in the play-off classic, Bearden was in rare form as he floated his knuckler through the stiff breeze blowing off Lake Erie. Gene gave up five hits, two of which were followed by double plays. The Indians could get only five hits, two by Bearden himself. Gene doubled in the third and scored on an error. In the fourth, a walk and singles by Robinson and Hegan made the score 2 to 0, and there it remained.

Boudreau came up with a surprise starter in the fourth

game. Steve Gromek, sidearming right-hander, had shown flashes of his old skill late in the season and Lou rewarded him with a World Series assignment before 81,897. For the second time, Southworth's pitcher was Sain, and for the second time Sain pitched beautifully. But this time he was not so fortunate as he was in Boston.

Mitchell's single and Boudreau's double netted a run in the first. In the third, Doby peeled off the first home run of the Series, a smash over the fence in right center. With those runs, Gromek outlasted Sain in a 2-to-1 game that was one of the best pitched and best played of the entire set.

Cleveland was running its highest baseball fever of a hectic season. The Indians were leading in the series, three games to one. It could be all over Sunday, October 10. Feller would try again. Lemon, Bearden, and Gromek had won World Series games. The king of the moderns, Feller, was due for his just reward.

The largest mass of humanity in the history of the game descended on the stadium. Close to eight thousand stood behind the outfield fence. Others stood in the stands or squatted on steps. The official count was 86,288!

Ironically, the biggest crowd saw the worst ball game. Obviously far off form, Feller lasted until the seventh. He managed to maintain a 5-5 tie until then, mainly because Nelson Potter, the Boston starter, had been chased in the fourth by Hegan's home run with two on. Mitchell had tagged Potter for a homer on the game's second pitch.

The Braves decided in the seventh to manhandle Feller and whoever followed him. Elliott had slammed two homers off Feller earlier. In a wild inning high-lighted by five singles, two walks, one error, and a balk by Satchel Paige, the fourth Cleveland pitcher of the day, the Braves scored six times, sewed up an 11-to-5 crushing conquest, and sent the Series back to Boston for conclusion.

The sixth and final game was the best of the entire Series. Lemon started after his second triumph and outpitched Voiselle for seven innings while 40,103 loyal New Englanders groaned. Mitchell and Boudreau doubled for one run in the third inning, but the Braves came back, with the equalizer in the fourth on Elliot's single, a walk, and Mike McCormick's single. Gordon opened the sixth with a home run, a mighty drive over the left-field fence. Then a walk, Robinson's single, and an infield out produced one more run. In the eighth, after Spahn had replaced Voiselle, the Tribe increased the lead to 4-1 on successive singles by Keltner, Tucker, and Robinson.

The World Series seemed to be all over right then, but the Braves promptly showed they were still in the ball game. Holmes singled. Torgeson scored him with a solid double to right. Lemon, unnerved, walked Elliot. Boudreau trotted to the pitching rubber, took the ball from Lemon, and signaled to the bull pen. In strolled the long, lean left-hander, Bearden, hero of many Boston incidents. But this wasn't the terrifying Bearden of before. Clint Conatser greeted Gene with a liner that rattled the glove of Tucker in center. Masi doubled, and Boudreau's jitters tripled. But Bearden himself tossed out the next batter and the pay-off battle moved into the ninth with the Tribe guarding a 4-to-3 lead.

Bearden walked the first Brave, Stanky, and Connie Ryan ran for him. Then Sibi Sisti, batting for Spahn, attempted to sacrifice. He popped a fifteen-footer in front of the plate. Hegan made a spectacular grab of the ball and then doubled the astonished Ryan off first base.

The Series was over; Cleveland had won!

But Bearden wasn't carried off the field this time. It had been a drab, wearisome World Series. The Indians had fought their big battles in the American League. These fusses with the National League were almost boring except for the money. The Indians collected 6,772 dollars each, a record pay-off, while the losing Braves were rewarded with 4,651 dollars apiece, a little under the highest previous total for a loser's share.

Bill  Veeck and Larry Doby

# Veeck on Doby

## by BILL VEECK with ED LINN

When I came to Cleveland, I was almost sure I was going to sign a Negro player. We had four or five Negro friends sending us reports from the beginning. At the start of the 1947 season, I hired a Negro public relations man, Lou Jones, so that he could familiarize himself with the league ahead of time and serve as a companion and a buffer to the player we signed. I spoke to the Negro leaders of the city and told them I was going to hold them responsible for policing their own people in case of trouble. (There was nothing for them to be responsible for, of course. We never had one fight in Cleveland in which a Negro was involved.)

I moved slowly and carefully, perhaps even timidly. It is usually overlooked, but if Jackie Robinson was the ideal man to break the color line, Brooklyn was also the ideal place. I wasn't that sure about Cleveland. Being unsure, I wanted to narrow the target areas as much as possible; I wanted to force the critics to make their attacks on the basis of pure prejudice—if they dared—and not on other grounds. To give them no opportunity to accuse us of signing a Negro as a publicity gimmick, I had informed the scouts that I wasn't necessarily looking for the best player with the best long-term potential. And I only wanted to sign one Negro  because, despite those glowing credentials I have given myself, I felt that I had to be in a position to extricate the club fairly easily in case we ran into too many problems.

The player whose name kept floating to the top was Larry Doby, the second baseman of the Newark Eagles.

I offered Mrs. Effa Manley, the owner of the Newark club, $10,000 for Doby's contract, plus an additional $10,000 if he made our team. Effa was so pleased that she told me I could have the contract of her shortstop, who she thought was just as good, for $1,000. Our reports on the shortstop were good too. We had eliminated him because we thought he was too old. To show how smart I am, the shortstop was Monte Irvin.

To make it as easy as possible for Doby, I decided to make the announcement on the road. Lou Jones picked him up in Newark and brought him to the Congress Hotel in Chicago to meet me and the press. In the taxi, on the way to the park, I told Larry, "If you have any troubles, come and talk them over with me. This is not the usual con, I mean this. It will take some time for the other fellows to get used to you. You have to accept that. You may have to go it alone for awhile. That's why Lou Jones is here."

A couple of the players made their objections known; I found faraway places to send them. Predictably, they were players of little talent and therefore the most threatened economically. Joe Gordon, a club leader, was the player who welcomed Doby with the most open heart and became his friend and confidant. That didn't surprise me at all. Some of the writers disapproved, although not in print and not to me personally. That did surprise me.

In his first day in uniform, July 3, 1947, Doby saw action as a pinch hitter and struck out. During that whole first year, he was a complete bust. The next year, however, when Tris Speaker and Bill McKechnie converted him into a centerfielder, Larry began to hit and one of our weak positions suddenly became one of our strongest.

Some of the players who had not seemed overjoyed at having Larry on the team became increasingly fond of him as it became apparent that he was going to help them slice a cut of that World Series money. The economics of prejudice, as I have discovered many times, cuts both ways.

And when Doby hit a tremendous home run to put us ahead in the fourth game of the World Series, it could be observed that none of the 81,000 people who were on their feet cheering seemed at all concerned about—or even conscious of—his color.

Doby was as close to me as any player I have ever known, although it took awhile before he would stop in the office to talk over his troubles. I am extremely fond of Larry and of his wife, Helyn, and their children. After all that is said, I have to add, in all honesty, that he was not the best man we could have picked for the first Negro player in the league. I don't say that from the club's point of view, since we could not have won without him, but from his.

Larry had been an all-sports star in Paterson, New Jersey. A local hero. He had never come face-to-face with prejudice until he became a big-leaguer. Prejudice was something he knew existed, something which he accommodated himself to in his youth if only in the knowledge that it was going to keep him out of organized baseball. He had not been bruised as a human being, though; he had not had his nose rubbed in it. It hit him late in life; it hit him at a time he thought he had it licked; and it hit him hard.

We did not train in Florida. I had moved our training quarters to Arizona, not so much in preparation for Doby as out of an unpleasant experience with the Milwaukee Brewers. The Brewers' regular training headquarters were in Ocala, Florida. Our clubhouse was way out in left field, and the Jim Crow section was between the clubhouse and the edge of the stands. I was rather naive about segregation. In those days it wasn't really publicized that much, as I suppose many Northern soldiers who took back seats in buses found out.

At Tucson, I discovered, the bleachers weren't segregated but the hotel was. We weren't able to talk the management into allowing Larry to stay with us his first year, although we did make it clear—and they agreed—that in the future they would take all of our players, regardless of race, creed or previous condition of servitude. It was easy enough for me to tell Larry that these things took time. It was true enough to say that we had, after all, broken through one color barrier even if he was going to have to wait a year. It was easy for me, because it was he who was being told to be patient and to wait.

But Larry was not a man to shake off those earlier slights and insults that easily. He was always very sensitive. If he wanted to dispute an umpire's call, he would back off and point to the back of his hand, as if to say, "You called that on me because I'm colored."

When he was knocked down, he would sometimes throw his bat out at the mound. There was no doubt, understand, that he was right in thinking he was being thrown at because he was colored. All colored players were thrown at for years, a practice arising from an old coach's tale that Negroes didn't have the guts to come up off the ground and dig back in. It is usually called, with a delicacy unusual in baseball, "taking their power away." (Here, again, notice the rationalization of an economic prejudice. Having drawn the color line, we had to tell ourselves that the Negro, after all, didn't have it in him to make the grade anyway.) Some of them, like Luke Easter, would get up laughing and, as often as not, knock the next pitch out of the park. Larry may have hit the next pitch out of the park, but he wasn't laughing.

It was a very real and bitter and gnawing battle for Larry all the way. He suffered such a shock that he was possessed by the idea that he had to fight the battle for his kids, Larry Jr. and Christine, so that they would never be bruised as badly as he had been.

With all that, his inner turmoil was such a constant drain on him that he was never able to realize his full potential. Not to my mind, at any rate. Not that he wasn't a very good player. He led the league in home runs twice. In 1954, when the Indians won the pennant, he led in both home runs and runs batted in. If Larry had come up just a little later, when things were just a little better, he might very well have become one of the greatest players of all time.

# Browns Rout Eagles in Their First

# NFL Contest

## by HAROLD SAUERBREI

### 9/50

Philadelphia, Sept. 16—The forward pass is a precious weapon and the Cleveland Browns demonstrated its usefulness as Greasy Neale's Philadelphia Eagles and 71, 237 fans in Municipal Stadium stared in open-mouthed wonder tonight.

Firm and poised at times, sometimes forced to hurry his throws but nearly always getting the ball away, Otto Graham conducted the Browns to their first victory in the National Football League, a convincing 35-to-10 triumph over the Eagles.

Thirty-eight times the deliberate Graham tossed the football in the air and on 21 occasions a list of receivers that included Mac Speedie, Dante Lavelli, Dub Jones, Rex Bumgardner and Marion Motley clutched the object as if it were the world's last loaf of bread.

By this simple expedient, the Browns defeated the two-time champions of the National League and established themselves as favorites to dominate activities among their new associates as they did in the old All-America Conference.

Graham got the Browns into a 21-3 lead with three touchdown passes—one each to Jones, Speedie and Lavelli—and then just to show the Browns can run with the ball, called on his running attack which responded with two more scores to complete the rout in the last three minutes of play.

Graham scored one of the final touchdowns on a sneak from the 1-yard line, while Bumgardner took a pitchout from Otto and raced wide around right end for 2 yards and the final

Paul Brown in the classroom

marker, which was set up by a 57-yard dash by Jones.

While the Browns' offensive specialists were throwing the ball and catching it deftly, the strongest running attack the National League has known in the last few years was of little worth against the rushes of Clyde (Smackover) Scott, Frank Ziegler and the other Eagle runners.

The Eagles, too, finally called on an aerial attack to get their only touchdown, which came on a 17-yard pass from Bill Mackrides to Pete Pihos, the veteran end.

After the contest, Pro Football Commissioner Bert Bell visited the Browns' dressing room and called the victors "the best football team I have ever seen."

Coach Paul Brown's reply to this glowing compliment was: "We are not going to gloat over this. There is a long season ahead."

That running attack by the Eagles, which was stopped with only 148 yards gained, was weakened by the absence of Steve Van Buren, and by the loss of Scott just before the half ended. Van Buren, who underwent a toe operation a month ago, was dressed but did not play, while Scott was jarred as he rammed into that stalwart Cleveland line and was taken to the hospital with a shoulder separation.

And that is the way the game was played all night—the athletes being as high spirited as school boys.

Not all the misfortune befell the Eagles, however. The first time the Browns touched the ball, Don Phelps caught a punt and ran 64 yards for a touchdown, but the play was called back and Cleveland penalized 15 yards for clipping.

The Browns not only were deprived of making their debut in this spectacular fashion, but lost Lou Groza, offensive left tackle and kicking specialist, as well. On the same play, Groza bruised his left arm while throwing a block and was lost for the game.

In his absence, Derrell Palmer went the route as offensive left tackle, John Kissell substituted for Palmer at defensive left tackle and Chubby Grigg became the conversion expert. Grigg, who never before had been a place-kicker, was successful five times, but missed a field goal from the 25.

Preceding Grigg's field goal try, made possible when Jim Martin recovered a Philadelphia fumble on the Eagles' 39, where Scott fumbled a punt by Gillom, the home team had taken a 3-0 lead on Patton's 17-yard field place kick.

After Grigg missed with his attempt, the Eagles took the ball on the 20, but failed to move and Frank Reagan directed another punt in Phelp's direction. Once more Phelps fielded the leather and headed for the goal line, running 46 yards before being stopped. But the Browns were offside. Reagan got another chance and this time punted a distance of 36 yards, the ball rolling out of bounds on the Cleveland 41.

As if exasperated by ill luck on Phelps' running, the Browns went to work in earnest. Graham took the ball from Center Frank Gatski, retreated into the pocket and waited for Jones to dart into the open.

When the tall right half got 10 yards behind all the Eagle defenders, Graham threw. Jones caught it and ran alone and undisturbed into the end zone, where Referee Bill Downes flung his arms in the air in traditional touchdown signal, sending the Browns off to a successful start in football's "big league."

An epidemic of fumbles broke out in the second period and two of them were by Motley. One fumble checked a scoring drive by the Browns, while the second set them in a hole.

But Motley redeemed himself when the Eagles got to the Browns' 3, where they had a first down. Three times Motley, who was inserted as a linebacker, met the Eagle ball carrier head on and three times the big fullback stopped the thrust short of the goal line.

Shortly after this display of defensive play, Cliff Lewis intercepted a pass by Tommy Thompson on his own 25 and returned four yards to the 39. Time was running out, but the Browns made it 14-3 before the half ended, with Graham throwing to Lavelli for 26 yards and the score.

Otto had not called on Lavelli as a receiver since early in the game, but this time Dante broke clear of his guard and took the throw while racing at top speed to the goal posts.

The Browns took the second-half kickoff, which went into the end zone. Starting from the 20, Graham began passing to Bumgardner, Lavelli and Speedie, and the Browns marched 80 yards for another touchdown.

The touchdown play was a 12-yard pass from Graham to Speedie, a play on which Graham got off a great pass with and Eagle lineman hanging onto him. Speedie made a leaping catch on the 2 and stepped across.

Then the Eagles came surging back. They started on a drive from their own 14, but were halted when Hal Herring intercepted a Thompson pass. A few plays later, Joe Sutton stole one of Graham's throws on his 45 and this led to the Eagles' lone touchdown, which made the score 21-10.

Philadelphia's hopes now were revived. But only briefly. Midway through the fourth period, the Browns got the ball on their own 46. Graham passed to Speedie for 14 yards and then turned the task over to the ball carriers.

The Browns ran seven straight times and made 28 yards to the Eagle 1, from where Graham stepped over on the sneak.

A few plays later, Warren Lahr intercepted a pass on his own 34. Jones took a handoff from Graham, swept wide around left end and proceeded for 57 yards before he was stopped at the 7. Jones was halted once near the line of scrimmage, but kept tugging, freed himself and broke away on the long dash. On fourth down from the 2, Bumgardner went around right end and over.

Graham's 21 pass completions were good for 346 yards. On 24 running attempts the Browns gained 141 yards which was only seven less than the Eagles made on 44 tries.

Lou Groza's winning field goal

# The Greatest Football Game,

# Browns Vs. Rams

## by JACK CLARY

## 12/50

The greatest football game? Most would nominate the 1958 championship, when the Colts beat the Giants in sudden-death overtime. But herewith a by-no-means lone vote for the 1950 championship tussle between the Browns and the Rams. The finest football teams functioned at their most brilliant, seemingly leaving nothing to chance and everything to skill, and neatly resolved the issue in the closing seconds. A perfect fit.

So often the matchups with the greatest excitement become resolute but essentially dull wars of attrition, as if each side fears the other too much to dare risk being great at its expense. Yet when the Browns and Rams battled in their first championship confrontation, every star shone at its brightest. And there were plenty of them—no less than eight who would later be elected to the Pro Football Hall of Fame: Otto Graham, Marion Motley, Bob Waterfield, Norm Van Brocklin, Tom Fears, Elroy Hirsch, Lou Groza, and Dante Lavelli.

How good were these teams? Some statistics: The Rams scored 466 points in 12 regular-season games, an average of nearly 40 points per contest. Their two quarterbacks, Waterfield and Van Brocklin, passed for 3,709 yards, or more than 300 yards per game. One week the Rams piled up 10 touchdowns and 70 points against Baltimore. The next they made 9 touchdowns and 65 points, including 41 points in the third quarter against Green Bay.

Unlike most teams, which needed to establish a running

game before they could pass effectively, the Rams unabashedly came out throwing. Fears caught 84 passes that season, including 7 for touchdowns. Not that the Rams couldn't run. Indeed they boasted two offensive backfields—the fast-striking unit of Glenn Davis, Verda ("Vitamin T") Smith, and Tom Kalminir, and "the Bull Elephant Backfield" of Paul ("Tank") Younger, Dan Towler, and Ralph Pasquariello.

Against this high-flying, the Browns pitted the best defense in the league—144 points in 12 games. Their offense had produced points at a less prolific rate than the Rams had, but quarterback Graham did not give away much to the Waterfield-Van Brocklin combination, or Speedie and Lavelli to Hirsch and Fears, or Motley and Rex Bumgardner to the Rams' backfields.

Other than Van Brocklin, who had broken ribs from the Rams' 24-14 playoff victory over Chicago, the arsenals of both clubs were ready for the battle on the frozen turf at Cleveland Stadium. Sure enough, the game began with a series of dazzling offensive explosions. Knowing that the Browns' defense would be concentrating on covering Hirsch and Fears, and that its linebackers would be keying on Smith, L.A. coach Joe Stydahar designed a play in which all three men were used as decoys. On the game's first play from scrimmage, the ends and the fullback started on patterns to the right while Davis stayed momentarily in the backfield as if to block. So conscious were the Browns of the Rams' power that they forgot about Davis. As they moved right to cover Hirsch, Fears, and Smith, Davis streaked down the left sideline, caught Waterfield's pass near midfield, and flew past Ken Gorgal and Tommy James of the Cleveland secondary on a 82-yard scoring play. Elapsed time: 27 seconds, and the Rams led 7-0.

It took the Browns six plays to get even. They covered 72 yards, 21 on runs by Graham and 31 on the scoring play—a strike from Graham to Jones. Groza converted and the game was tied.

Then it was the Rams' turn again. Waterfield hit Fears twice, once on a 44-yard pass. From the 19 Smith charged around left end to the 4. Then, on the eighth play of the drive, Hoerner slammed over tackle for the score. The extra point made it Rams 14, Browns 7.

Three series, three touchdowns, on a total of 15 plays from scrimmage. Not many contests can match that for an opening fusillade. And rather than deteriorate into a ragged, high-scoring free-for-all, as some contests do when points come quickly and easily at the outset, this one emulated and eventually surpassed the taut precision of those opening drives.

The Browns returned the Rams' kickoff to the 35. A pass interference call against Woodley Lewis on Speedie and a 17-yard completion to Speedie moved the ball to the Los Angeles 26. From there Graham went to Lavelli for the score with less than four minutes gone in the second quarter.

Just when the carving up of the defenses seemed effortless, an inexplicable lapse on the most routine play in football, the conversion, seemed to change the game's character. A high snap from center Hal Herring caused James to fumble the extra-point placement, and his desperation pass into the end zone was dropped.

Now the defenses gradually reawakened. The Rams reached the Cleveland 7, only to be waylaid by a penalty and thwarted by a pass interception. Then the Rams' defense stiffened and regained the ball on the Cleveland 46. Waterfield marched his men to a first down on the 12, but Cleveland smothered three plays for only four yards, and Waterfield, though the wind was behind him, missed a 15-yard field goal. The offenses, which minutes before had appeared irrestible, now had strangely subsided, and the defenses assumed control of the game.

For Cleveland Len Ford led the defensive charge. Having missed most of the season with a fractured jaw, and still fifteen pounds under his playing weight, Ford had come in as a replacement for rookie defensive end Jim Martin, whom the Rams had victimized for sizable gains in their opening drives. On three consecutive plays, Ford threw Smith for a 14-yard loss on a reverse, sacked Waterfield for an 11-yard loss, and threw Davis for a 13-yard loss on a sweep. Total: 38 yards in three plays. The Browns' defense seemed to have solidified.

Before the first half ended, Graham sent the Browns ahead 20-14 on a touchdown pass to Lavelli, capping a superbly executed 77-yard drive. The Rams answered midway in the third quarter with two touchdowns within 25 seconds and took a seemingly invincible 28-20 lead. First, Waterfield passed 38 yards to Smith to the Browns' 17-yard line. Hoerner then ran at Cleveland's defense seven straight times until he scored on fourth down from the 1-yard line. On the Browns' first running play after the kickoff, Motley—swarmed over all this cold day by the aggressive Los Angeles defense—lost the ball. End Larry Brink scooped it up at the 6-yard line and easily scored the second touchdown.

Paul Brown had inured his team to such sudden turnabouts. There was no question of panic or hopelessness. Brown prepared his great players so thoroughly that they could not easily conceive of an insurmountable obstacle. Surely an eight-point deficit with a quarter left to play did not qualify. Defensive back Warren Lahr began the Browns' third and final comeback of the game. He intercepted Waterfield's pass some five minutes into the fourth quarter and Graham began to peck away at the Rams' defense. Otto had been magnificent most of this afternoon but now he outdid himself. On a fourth-and-four situation he passed for seven yards. On a fourth-and-three he ran for the first down. Finally, on the eighth play of this fine drive, he passed to Bumgardner, who, foiling Woodley Lewis' perfect coverage, made a diving catch just inside the end zone. Groza's kick narrowed the Rams' lead to 28-27.

Graham got the ball back four plays later and with three minutes to play marched Cleveland to within field goal distance. Not content to allow Groza to kick from near the 30-yard line, Graham sprinted for a first down to keep the drive going. As he tried to dance and dodge for another precious yard or two, Milan Lazetich, the big linebacker, blindsided Graham, caused him to fumble, and then recovered the ball. "I never saw the guy coming," Graham would say later. "I wanted to dig a hole right in the middle of that stadium, crawl into it and bury myself forever. I got to the sidelines and wanted to hide. But Paul came over, put his arm around my shoulder and said, 'Don't worry. We'll get it back. We'll win this thing yet.' He told me later he really meant it, that he wasn't just trying to make me feel good."

The Rams needed but one first down and the game was theirs. But the Browns' defense struck down Hoerner on two straight runs for no gain, then collared Glenn Davis after he made six yards off tackle.

The fans who had begun to stream to the exit portals stopped for one last look, then continued home when Waterfield boomed a 51-yard kick against the wind. Cliff Lewis caught the ball at his 19-yard line and ran out of bounds after progressing to the 32. A minute and 50 seconds remained and the Browns were 68 yards from the Los Angeles end zone.

Graham forgot his despair. This last, desperate drive began when Otto could find no open receivers and ran 14 yards to the Browns' 46-yard line. Then his passing game came alive—15 yards to Bumgardner in the left flat, 16 yards to Jones in the right flat. There was one minute to play as the ball rested on the Los Angeles 23-yard line.

The imperturbable Graham, confidently in control now, found Bumgardner again, this time for 12 yards to the Los Angeles 11. Graham called timeout and went to the sidelines for Brown's counsel. Upstairs in the coaches' booth, assistant Blanton Collier had been watching each play unfold. As he considered Groza's field-goal kicking, he was bothered by the brisk right-to-left crosswind that swept the open end of the stadium, towards which his team was driving.

"The ball had been marked on the left hashmark when Otto called a timeout, and this left a bit of an angle," Collier still remembers. "Paul came to the phone and said, 'What do you think?'

"I said, 'Let's run Otto on a quarterback sneak to the right because of that wind, then kick it.' He said, 'Okay.'

"I lived one hundred years for the next few seconds because all of a sudden it dawned on me, 'You crazy nut! You have the ball down there now and you want to take a chance on someone fumbling it on this frozen ground just to move it in a little better position.' That's all we would get, maybe just a little better position. But I had become so intent on that factor I forgot about the danger of handling the football in one more scrimmage situation."

But Graham was not about to fumble again. After he gained even better position than Collier had hoped for, he called timeout again. Now it was up to Groza, who stood near the spot where Waterfield earlier had missed a 15-yard field goal. "The only thing I thought about was my own little checklist for kicking a ball," Groza says. "I didn't hear the crowd, I blotted out the distance, the time left, even the score. All I had to do was kick the ball."

And he did. Straight and true, sixteen yards into that tricky wind and through the iron pipes. As the ball soared upward, twenty-two players froze in a bizarre tableau. Once they heard the thud of Groza's famed toe against the ball, there was nothing to do but watch.

Only 28 seconds remained to be played. Cleveland could not have cut it much closer.

# Giants Sweep Indians

## by HARRY JONES

## 10/54

The New York Giants are the newly crowned champions of the baseball world and no one—certainly not the Cleveland Indians—can challenge their authority.

They ascended the throne in true championship style, convincingly defeating the Indians in the fourth straight game yesterday, 7-4, before a crowd of 78,102 fans at the stadium.

Manager Leo Durocher's Giants, an 18-10 underdog at the start, brought the National League its first world title since 1946 and became the first National League club to win four straight since 1914.

With better pitching, better defense and far greater power, the Giants completely ruined whatever hope for immortality the Indians had cherished after setting a new American League record with 111 victories.

They won the final game by driving Bob Lemon from the mound in the fifth inning, by assuming a 7-0 lead in that inning, and by turning back the rallies the Indians mustered late in the encounter.

Pinch hitters drove in the Indians' only runs. Hank Majeski walloped a three-run homer over the left field fence off little Don Liddle, the Giants' winning pitcher, and Rudy Regalado singled a run across off the same southpaw.

But when the Indians began other attacks the Giants called upon Hoyt Wilhelm, who stopped them with the potential tying run at bat in the seventh, and then upon Johnny Antonelli, who stopped them in a similar situation in the eighth.

With two men on base and one out in the eighth, Antonelli struck out Vic Wertz, who had made two hits, and curved a called third strike past Wally Westlake.

He walked Sam Dente, leading off the ninth, but retired the last three men in order.

Jim Hegan fouled out, Pinch Hitter Dave Philley struck out and then Dale Mitchell, another pinch hitter, swung at an outside pitch and raised a short foul near third base. Hank Thompson raced over and grabbed it for the last out of the 1954 World Series.

The Giants, with a perfect right to celebrate their clean sweep, mobbed Antonelli.

Pounding him on the back, pumping his hand, they escorted him from the field and into the clubhouse where they practically raised the roof in a scene of great jubilation.

This was the first World Series championship for the Giants since 1933, when a team managed by Bill Terry defeated the Washington Nationals in five games. It was the fifth victory in the history of the Giants, who have been on the losing side nine times.

It was the first World Series victory for a National League club since the St. Louis Cardinals defeated the Boston Red Sox in 1946. The New York Yankees had won six world titles in the last seven years—five in succession—and the Indians had won one.

It was the first four-game sweep by a National League club since 1914, when George Stallings' Boston Braves, in last place on July 4, won the pennant and then defeated the Philadelphia Athletics. No National League team had done it before.

It was also the first World Series victory for Durocher; he had made two attempts to defeat the Yankees. He lost as manager of the Giants in 1941.

After winning by scores of 5-2 and 3-1 in the Polo Grounds and by a 6-2 count here Friday, the Giants made up their minds that this would be the last one. They scored two runs in the second inning, one in the third and then four in the fourth.

The Indians must have decided this would be the last one, too. They got only one hit off Liddle in four innings, a double by (who else?) Vic Wertz. Two Giant errors were made with two out in the fifth and then Majeski gave the Tribe a moment of futile hope.

Swinging at Liddle's second pitch, Hank sent a drive to left which barely cleared the fence. It was the fifth pinch home run in World Series history and the second of this series. Dusty Rhodes broke up the opener with one off Lemon in the 10th inning.

Two Cleveland errors helped the Giants score their two runs in the second inning. Wertz made a wild throw and Westlake, a flop both at bat and in the field, dropped an easy fly ball.

The rally started when Hank Thompson walked. Monte Irvin doubled to the fence in left-center, Thompson stopping at third, and then Davey Williams hit a liner to Wertz. Vic uncorked a wild throw to second trying to double Irvin.

Thompson scored from third on the error and Irvin moved to third. West Westrum then hit a fly to right field which Westlake dropped as he was about to throw home. Irvin scored on the sacrifice fly and Westrum was ruled safe at first base.

Alvin Dark singled to left with one out in the third and then took third as Don Mueller singled to right. Willie Mays bounced a double over Al Rosen's head at third base, Dark scoring and Mueller pulling up at third.

An intentional walk to Thompson filled the bases and brought up Irvin. Instead of using Dusty Rhodes as a pinch hitter in this spot, as he had in the first three games, Durocher let Irvin bat and he struck out. The rally came to a close.

But the Giants started another in the fifth. Dark again sent a single to left. Mueller singled, Dark taking third, and Mays walked on five pitches, filling the bases.

Lemon was removed by Manager Al Lopez and Hal Newhouser came in.

The veteran southpaw walked Thompson, forcing Dark across and then served a single to Irvin, scoring Mueller and Mays. Thompson stopped at second on the hit, but moved to third on a sacrifice by Williams and scored on another sacrifice fly by Westrum.

Up to this point the Indians had made only one hit. Wertz had doubled to the fence in right-center after (1) arguing he had been hit on the right hand by a pitched ball, and (2) hitting a fly to left which dropped foul, a matter of inches from the line.

With two away in the fifth, Dente reached first safely when Liddle, covering first on his grounder to Whitey Lockman, missed the bag for an error at second base by Williams, who muffed a grounder.

Majeski then connected, leaving the Indians with a four-run deficit but instilling new hope.

The side went out in order in the sixth inning and then Wertz started a rally in the seventh by slashing a single to center—his eighth hit in 15 times at bat.

Westlake struck out, Dente flied out and Hegan singled to left, Wertz stopping at second. Regalado was inserted here as a pinch hitter for Don Mossi and he singled through the box, scoring Wertz and moving Hegan to third base.

Durocher removed Liddle and brought in Wilhelm to pitch to Al Smith. But Manager Lopez took Smith out and inserted the left-handed hitting Dave Pope, who had hit Wilhelm hard in springtime exhibitions. This time, though, Pope tapped to the mound.

Bob Avila reached first on an unusual error as the lead-off batter in the Cleveland eighth. Swinging at a wide-breaking knuckle ball, Avila missed completely for strike three. But the ball got past Westrum. Avila ran to first and Wilhelm got the error.

Larry Doby flied out and Rosen followed with a single to left, Avila taking third. But the left-handed Antonelli entered here, struck out Wertz and got Westlake on a called third strike. He was equally as difficult in the ninth inning.

The Giants got only two hits and no runs in the last four innings off Mossi and Mike Garcia. The damage, however, had been done. And a lasting damage it was.

# Graham's Swan Song, Another

# Title

## by JAMES E. DOYLE

### 12/55

DON'T SAY IT TO THE BROWNS

Who says there ain't no
    Santa Claus?
Just listen to the Browns'
    haw-haws!
        —Lake Shore Liner.

\*    \*    \*    \*    \*

The Browns made Santa come to them, and even as the old chimney whiz answered their call, the roof fell in on the Los Angeles Rams.

PERFECT

'Twas the day after Christmas,
    and I heard Paul Brown say,
"Perfect day for a slaughter—
    of Rams in L. A."
        —Egg Shelley.

GOLD COAST

Just a California gold coast it was, for the Browns . . .
A coast, that is, to the fattest pot of gold ever hung up for

41

Otto Graham's last championship performance

this world's professional football championship.

WORD FROM THE WISE

Whenever those blue chips
    are down,
The wise men crack, just
    stick with Brown.
          —Lank Fellow.

\*   \*   \*   \*   \*

That massive Los Angeles Coliseum wasn't built for a slaughter house, but it served the purpose nicely.

RIGHT PITCH AGAIN

Otto Graham, the retirin'est guy in all football history, had the proper pitch for his swan song once more.

\*   \*   \*   \*   \*

And when he wasn't running up the score with his pitches, he was running it up—period.

HOT DOGGEREL

Ot's never hotter with his firing
Than on those days when he's retiring.
          —Hedge Pufflefinger.

\*   \*   \*   \*   \*

"But I'm not going to have any more retire trouble," said the post-graduate pass master after he had left the scene of the action late in the afternoon, with the folks giving him the

Hand of the Year for Christmas. "This is really it."

## A DON PAUL ON EACH SIDE

There were two Don Pauls in the game, one on each side . . . But you can bet that Paul Brown wouldn't take five Ram Pauls for the Brown Paul, who was off and running 65 yards for the first of the champions' five touchdowns after neglecting to beg Skeets Quinlan's pardon for spearing a forward pass that Norm Van Brocklin had aimed at the steaming Skeets.

## LUKEWARM DOGGEREL

"The whole Brown club was too
     alert,"
The Rams' fans moaned. "And did that
     hurt!"
                    —Beau Ling Greenstein.

\*    \*    \*    \*    \*

On their toes and on the ball—that was the Browns—and on the happiest belated Christmas celebration, last night, that you could wish to see . . . Not to mention hear.

## SAM CLICKS IN CLUTCH

Injured in the first 30 seconds of action, Chuck Noll, the Browns' crack linebacker, was a Chuck null and void thereafter . . . But stalwart Sam Palumbo, an Irish-bred freshman who'd thought he was just along for the ride, stepped in there as Chuck's replacement, rode one after another Los Angeles ball-carrier into the turf and intercepted a forward heave, to boot . . . He nestled the ball to his bosom, though, as happily as you please, instead of booting.

## TWAIN MET AND—WHAM!

Oh, east is east and west is
    west,
As Mr. Kipling said.
And who doubts now that east is
    best
And it will stay ahead?
                —Bard of Avon-on-Lake.

Herb Score is struck in the eye.

# Score Hit in Eye

## by CHUCK HEATON
## 5/57

Felled by a vicious line drive that struck him squarely in the right eye last night at the Stadium, Herb Score lies in Lakeside Hospital today with his baseball future clouded.

His vision is impaired due to severe hemorrhaging and extent of the damage will not be known for several days.

The Indians' 23-year-old ace left hander collapsed when the liner off the bat of the Yankees' Gil McDougald crashed against his head in the first inning. He did not lose consciousness, but bled profusely from the nose and eye.

Dr. Don Kelly, team physician, made the initial examination at the stadium after Score was carried off the field on a stretcher. Then Dr. Charles Thomas, Cleveland eye specialist, was called in for another examination at the hospital.

"He has light perception in that eye," Dr. Thomas said. "We can't do anything more until the hemorrhaging stops.

"He could be perfectly all right, but we just won't know for two or three days."

Score was in an amazingly cheerful mood as he waited for the ambulance in the hushed Cleveland dressing room and later at the hospital as he listened to the radio report of the Indians' 2-1 victory over New York.

"I didn't see the ball until it got a foot or two from my face," Herb recalled. "Then I saw too much of it. I never did lose consciousness even as I fell to the ground.

"I knew I was on the ground and I could feel the blood. Then people seemed to come at me from all sides. That Rocky (Colavito) must have set a new record getting in from right field."

Colavito and Score came up through the minor league ranks together and are particularly close buddies.

47

"Everybody started shoving towels at me and one even got in my mouth," Herb continued. "I almost choked on it."

The young southpaw thought the drive, which hit him with a sickening sound that sent a shudder through the crowd, touched his glove.

"I may be wrong but I think it just ticked the edge," Herb recalled.

"The pitch was right down the middle, maybe a little low. It was probably was straight as a string and came back the same way."

The ball caromed off Score's eye over to Al Smith, playing third base, and McDougald was thrown out. Manager Casey Stengel of the Yankees and Kerby Farrell, the Cleveland pilot, rushed to Score's aid as well as players from both teams.

Trainer Wally Bock gave first aid and a call went out over the public address system for a doctor. Several came down from the stands, but it was Dr. Kelly who supervised the move to the dressing room.

General Manager Hank Greenberg and Nate Dolin, a vice president, were in the Cleveland clubhouse when the initial examination was made. Then one hour after he had thrown the first pitch to open the ball game, Herb was in the hospital.

The pitched that was lined by McDougald was Herb's 12th of the night. He had retired Hank Bauer, the leadoff batter, and had a 2-2 count on McDougald.

Gil, the Yankee shortstop, was in tears after the game. He sat in a corner of the New York quarters and wiped his eyes with a towel as the other players dressed.

He asked for Dr. Kelly's telephone number, and it was reported that he hoped to visit Score at the hospital.

Herb told reporters that he had been struck several times before but only once on the head. That was during his high school pitching days at Lake Worth, Florida.

"It wasn't right in the eye like this," he recalled. "It sort of bounced off the forehead."

Greenberg and Tris Speaker, one of the pitcher's close friends and advisers, were at the hospital soon after Score's arrival.

Score's fiance, Nancy McNamara, was notified at St. Mary's College in Notre Dame, Indiana, and she may come to Cleveland today.

Herb, rated as one of the top pitchers in baseball, was the object of a reported million-dollar bid by the Boston Red Sox during spring training. He had won two games and lost one this season and before last night's game, Stengel had admitted that a loss to Herbie would come as no surprise.

Tough luck has dogged Herb most of his life. At the age of three he was hit by a truck and both his legs were crushed. For a time it was feared that he wouldn't walk normally.

As a youngster he had severe cases of pneumonia and rheumatic fever. Later he was hospitalized with a broken ankle and acute appendicitis.

Since he started playing professional baseball after signing with the Indians in 1952, Score hasn't had a season in which he wasn't sidelined. Last summer he was sidelined for a time with a stomach ailment. Two years back—his first with the Tribe—Score was laid up with a virus infection.

A dislocated collar bone halted him at Reading, Pennsylvania, in 1953, and the next year he suffered another attack of pneumonia in the final week of the season after winning 22 games for Indianapolis. During the 1957 spring training season the southpaw was bothered by a sore knee.

Score's injury brought to mind the one suffered by Early Wynn last summer in Washington. A line drive hit the burly pitcher on the jaw and it required 16 stitches to repair the damage. Big Gus was knocked unconscious, but didn't go down.

"You just have to try to get the glove up there and hope," Wynn recalled. "Some of them come back so fast you're helpless."

Wynn was back on the mound almost without losing a turn, and the baseball world hopes Score, one of its finest both off and on the field, enjoys the same good fortune.

Rocky Colavito (The Rock)

# Rocky Smacks Four Homers in

# One Game

## by GORDON COBBLEDICK

It was no secret that the Cleveland general manager, Frank Lane, wasn't numbered among the members of the Rocky Colavito Fan Club. It surprised no one, therefore, though it disturbed thousands, when rumors were heard in the early weeks of the 1958 season and in the winter following that he was trying to make a trade for the city's baseball hero. It was well authenticated that he had offered the Rock to Washington in exchange for pitcher Pedro Ramos and outfielder Jim Lemon and that only the Senators' rejection of the proposal kept it from being fact.

Shortly thereafter he suggested to the Detroit Tigers that it would be nice if they would deal Al Kaline to him for Colavito and a young outfielder named Roger Maris. The Tigers turned it down on the ground that Maris was scarcely more than an untested rookie and that, for all they knew, Colavito was a one-year flash, whereas Kaline was an established star.

Whatever disposition Detroiters might have had to deplore the decision when Maris broke Babe Ruth's long-standing record by hitting sixty-one homers as a member of the Yankees in 1961 was tempered by the fact that Rocky then was a member of the Tigers, for whom he socked forty-five.

Cleveland fans were less restrained. They called attention to the fact that their compulsive trader had swapped away 106 home runs and had, to show for them, only the twenty-eight contributed to the Indians' cause by Woodie Held and Vic Power, whom Lane had obtained from Kansas City in exchange for Maris.

51

Frantic Frankie had little patience with holdouts, and after his difference of opinion with Colavito in the matter of the latter's worth trade rumors again were current. They increased in number when Rock got off to a bad start in 1959, as he had in several earlier seasons.

A few minutes before the Indians took the field against the Orioles in Baltimore on June 10, five days before the legal deadlines for trades, Joe Gordon called him aside.

"Some screwball writer," said the manager, "has printed a story that we're going to trade you to the Red Sox. I want you to know it's a phony. I'd be crazy to approve a deal like that. You'd kill us in Fenway Park. In fact, I wouldn't trade you anywhere. But"—and here Gordon glared with mock ferocity—"I'll tell you something, Buster. If you don't start hitting pretty soon I'll send you back to Reading."

Rocky laughed.

"Reading's a good town, Skip," he said. "But don't worry. I'll hit. Only thing is you'll have to settle for singles today. Nobody hits home runs in this ball park."

Baltimore's Memorial Stadium was, in truth, conceded to be the "toughest home run park in baseball." Though the fences are only 309 feet from home plate on the foul lines, they fall away so sharply that the measurement in left and right center is 380. Since Baltimore's return to the major leagues in 1954 no man ever hit more than two homers in a game played there and no team ever had produced more than three.

Before that tenth day of June Rocky had made only four hits in his last thirty times at bat and had delivered only one home run since the first of the month. Other members of the team had been doing little better. Frank Lane had ordered twenty-five tennis rackets which he proposed to present to the Indians as a token of his contempt for their batting prowess.

In the first inning of that day's game the Rock worked pitcher Jerry Walker for a base on balls and scored when Minnie Minoso came out of his personal slump and blasted a homer into the left field seats.

In the bottom of the second he chased a fly by the Orioles' Billy Klaus close to the stands in the right-field corner and was doused with a cup of beer thrown by a hostile rooter.

"It made me kinda sore," he admitted later. "I mean I've nothing against beer taken internally in small amounts, but I don't want to bathe in it. I saw the guy that threw it, too, and I knew I'd recognize him if I ever saw him again."

In the third inning, with Walker still pitching, Rocky lofted a rather modest 365-foot fly that, being fairly close to the left-field foul line, cleared the fence for a homer. He was rewarded with a loud Bronx cheer by the beer-throwing fan when he took his defensive position for the next half-inning.

In the fifth, with Arnold Portocarrero on the mound for the Orioles, he slammed a 400-footer into the bleachers in left center—a drive that went unacknowledged by the beer thrower.

In the sixth Portocarrero delivered a fast ball, low and away, and the Rock drove it into the seats in center field, 420 feet away from the plate. It earned him a generous round of applause from the well-filled stands, the occupants of which were aware that they had seen local history made. A man had done what no other man ever had accomplished. Rocky Colavito had hit three home runs in one game in the "toughest home run park in baseball."

In the ninth, with Ernie Johnson pitching, he climaxed a historic day by driving one high into the left-center-field bleachers, 425 feet away.

This time he received a standing ovation. It was still at its thunderous height when he returned to his position in right field, and among the most vocal cheerers was the man who had tossed the beer.

"He even waved at me," Rocky reported, "and then I wasn't mad any more."

In all baseball's annals only seven other men ever had hit four home runs in one game. (An eighth was added when Willie Mays duplicated the feat two years later.) But of them all only two had done it in consecutive times at bat. They were

Bobby Lowe of the Boston National League club, who rapped four homers in successive at-bats in 1894, seven years before the American came into being, and Lou Gehrig of the Yankees, who did it in 1932.

It must be set down, too, that only Rocky Colavito racked up the record in a stadium whose contours were noted for discouraging home run hitting. The dimensions of the Boston park in 1894 are lost in the mists of time, but the Yankee Stadium in Gehrig's day, as now, was the softest touch of all for left-handed power hitters, among whom Babe Ruth and Roger Maris are counted.

Rocky's slugging that day paced the Indians to an 11-to-8 victory. Above the tumult in the clubhouse after the game a teammate shouted, "Now I suppose we gotta quit callin' you Joe D. From now on you're Babe R."

Another interposed an objection. "Babe Ruth never hit no four homers in one game. Neither did this Joe D.—this DiMaggio."

"Yeah, I guess you're right," the other agreed. "We'll just have to stick to 'Don't knock the Rock.' Whadaya say, gang? Let's hear it. Don't knock the Rock."

# A Hero Is Traded, Colavito for Kuenn

## by FRANK GIBBONS
### 4/60

When Frank Lane knocked the Rock by trading him to the Tigers yesterday for Harvey Kuenn, the telephone at The Press became almost too hot to handle.

I believe it was a dangerous deal, but I can't agree with a vast majority of the callers who rate it a total loss. Kuenn, after all, is an established major league star and it was surprising how many people failed to recall that he was the American League batting champion last season. He batted .353 to Colavito's .257.

In other words, Lane didn't trade Colavito for a bale of hay. He got a valuable ball player for him, one who can play centerfield acceptably, and do a number of things Rocky can't do.

Naturally, if Rocky hits 60 home runs and knocks in 125 runs for the Tigers, which is not beyond belief when he will play 77 games in Briggs Stadium, then Lane will have made a bad deal. I imagine the tar and feather group would swing into action.

If, however, Kuenn gets close to 200 hits and knocks in as many as 88 runs, which he did in 1956, then I think Lane will have made a fine swap. Then it will be surprising how many people thought it was a fine transaction right from the start.

Several callers made an important point in the deal which nobody can deny. Colavito undoubtedly is a better drawing card than Kuenn, because the man who hits the long ball has been of more interest ever since Babe Ruth. Kuenn's contribution

55

Angry fans demonstrate against the Colavito/Kuenn trade outside the Stadium.

must make the Indians a winner or there will be torpor at the turnstiles.

The Colavito supporters feel that Lane gave up too much power for Kuenn. This could be, only it is interesting to note that in last year's slugging records (times at bat into total bases) Colavito was fourth with .512, and Kuenn wasn't far behind, sixth with .501. He hits as many doubles as Colavito does home runs.

Kuenn doesn't strike out half as many times, he grounds into fewer double plays, and he is a speedier base runner, although not famous for this specialty.

Boil it all down and what you have left is that Lane gambled on a more complete player for a man with awesome power, a man who proved he could hit four home runs in one game in a place such as Baltimore's big park.

One thing we have to admit in this latest Lane marketing adventure is that he proved more than in any deal before that he has the guts of a burglar. Colavito, with his legions of power struck fans, could make Opening Day almost Closing Day for our fearless Frankie. A home run or two in the right places would do it.

It is possible, although I don't know this for certain, that Walter Bond figured largely in the thinking that preceded this deal. Bond will play right field tomorrow instead of center, a much easier assignment for a raw rookie. Lane also must believe that what the slugging Bond did in spring training will continue, and that because of this could afford to give up Colavito's crunching power.

That's a very long shot, of course, but Lane is always looking for a good price.

The departure of Colavito breaks up one of the most celebrated Damon and Pythias acts baseball has ever known. Herb Score and Rocky have been as close as brothers since their days at Indianapolis, and I find myself wondering if this may have entered into Lane's thinking.

"We will have 23 players plus Colavito and Score, who live

in their own world," was a Lane spring training comment. Lane has been discussing a trade for Score with several clubs, including Chicago.

It also is possible that Lane likes Kuenn because he chews tobacco and doesn't drink chocolate sodas. Lane doesn't like "chocolate soda" players.

I don't believe the age differential is very important in this deal. Kuenn is 29 and will become 30 in December. Colavito is 26 and will become 27 in August. It is entirely possible that Kuenn will outlast Rocky, although nobody can be certain of this and the percentage must be figured the other way. At any rate, for this season and several to come, I don't believe the ages matter.

No matter what we think of the deal, I believe we must admit that no more intriguing piece of business has been consummated in baseball for many seasons. Two stars are traded and play against each other on Opening Day. I don't recall this happening before.

I would imagine the deal would be hailed as a success in Detroit, where interest in the team has grown stagnant. Rocky could be as big as power steering in auto town.

# Ernie Davis, A Dream

# Unfulfilled

## by BILL SCHOLL
### 5/63

Ernie Davis, the All-American halfback from Syracuse, died today at Lakeside Hospital from leukemia without realizing his greatest dream—playing professional football.

A year ago at this time the quiet, smiling and always pleasant Davis was on the threshold of his most exciting years. He had a three-year, no-cut contract with the Browns calling for $65,000 plus a $15,000 bonus and training camp was only a few months away.

He never quite made it.

Instead, his dream ended with unexpected suddenness at 1 a.m. today after a 9 1/2 month battle with the blood disease. The 23-year-old athlete will be buried in Elmira, New York, his home town since he was a youngster, early next week.

Davis had been working for a soft drink company out of Cleveland until two days ago. He stopped in at the Browns' offices at the Stadium on Thursday morning and told Art Modell, the club president, that he was going into the hospital for several days.

Ernie had been making periodic trips to the hospital for blood checks and drug treatments.

"Ernie said he felt pretty good and would see us again shortly," said Modell, who had been very close to Davis the past 17 months.

Dr. Austin S. Weisberger, professor of medicine at Western Reserve University and one of the nation's outstanding authorities on blood disorders, said Davis died without any

59

What might have been—the dream backfield of Jim Brown and Ernie Davis (right)

discomfort.

Dr. Weisberger and Dr. Vic Ippolito, the Browns' team physician, had been watching over Davis since the disease was discovered last July.

It was while Davis was practicing with the College All-Stars under Otto Graham at Northwestern University late last July that he was found to have leukemia. There was no previous indication he was ill, although he had not distinguished himself in another all-star game at Buffalo a month earlier.

He mentioned that some wisdom teeth bothered him while attending the Browns' quarterback school at Hiram in early July and the teeth were extracted at Evanston a few weeks later.

Davis experienced some swelling about the neck glands after visiting the dentist and was hospitalized July 30 with what at first was thought to be mumps. Instead, leukemia was found.

He spent more than a month in hospitals in Evanston, Cleveland and Maryland, but was released early in September and began light workouts at League Park in October. He never was placed on the Browns' roster, but got some satisfaction in associating with the players at practice and on the bench at home games.

Ernie's blood count was completely normal from early fall until mid-winter and he kept in condition by sprinting, jogging and playing basketball. He experienced a flare-up in January and the treatments were stepped up for a time.

Of late, Ernie had been reported holding his own and remained active by studying Browns' films and traveling around Ohio for the soft drink firm.

Davis was probably the most heralded football player ever to come out of college. But he earned national recognition even before that as an all-around athlete at Elmira Free Academy.

"Ernie is next door to a legend," once said Marty Harrigan, his high school grid coach.

At Syracuse, Davis surpassed most of the records set by Jim

Brown and became the first Negro winner of the coveted Heisman Trophy.

He weighed 215 pounds and was the big back Paul Brown, then head coach of the Browns, wanted at halfback. To get the negotiating rights for Davis, Brown went out on a limb and gave up the fleet Bobby Mitchell and draftee Leroy Jackson to the Washington Redskins.

Davis was born in Uniontown, Pennsylvania, December 14, 1939. His father died when he was very young, and he lived with grandparents for a number of years while his mother went to Elmira to find employment and eventually remarry. She's now Mrs. Arthur Radford.

Ernie was reunited with his mother as a seventh-grader and they lived directly across the street from the high school at which he later starred.

"As a youngster, he was very shy and bashful, except when he was with close friends," said his mother at the time of signing with the Browns. "He was a very patient boy. I could always reason with him. Being an only child you'd think he might have been spoiled, but he wasn't.

"He was always very interested in school and never wanted to miss a day. He had to plug for grades, though, especially in junior and senior high."

Ernie weighed 140 pounds when he was 13 and was considered too big to carry the ball in Elmira's Small Fry League. So he dutifully took the role of a tackle.

He broke a wrist in his very first varsity game as a freshman and missed the entire season. When the basketball season came around he still had his wrist in a splint, but insisted on practicing and in the first game scored 22 points one-handed.

From then on, nothing could stop him in high school or college.

Upon heading for Syracuse he already was being mentioned in the same breath with Jim Brown and he remarked:

"I wish they wouldn't compare us. Naturally, I'd like to be an All-American and right now I'm hoping and praying that

I'll be able to go on . . . like Jim Brown . . . and play pro football. But after all, I'm just getting out of high school. I've still got to prove myself."

Ernie did prove himself and the proudest moment for him and his mother came when he signed with the Browns. His dream wasn't realized, but he never complained. He just went on hoping.

One memory stands out above all others regarding Ernie. It was the August night last year when 77,000 fans at the Stadium football double-header gave him a thunderous standing ovation as he walked to midfield alone under the glare of spotlights to be introduced.

It was as close as he ever got to his dream.

Fred Glover (#9) forcing the action

# Barons Win Calder Cup

## by THOMAS PLACE

### 4/64

The Cleveland Barons, labeled as rag-tags by their rivals before the start of the season, today are Calder Cup champions of the American Hockey League.

The battling Barons, playing every game as if their individual lives depended upon a victory, last night exploded for a 5-2 victory over the Quebec Aces before an overthrow throng of 10,016 at the Arena. The triumph was the Barons' ninth straight in the playoffs—the first time this most difficult feat ever has been accomplished.

The championship came as a great surprise, since the Barons finished third in the Western Division of the AHL and were underdogs in every series along the playoff trail.

But they outfought everyone, clipping Rochester in two straight, Hershey in three straight and finally the mighty Aces in four straight.

As the final seconds were ticking off the clock, the massive crowd gave its hockey heroes a standing ovation and the cheers were loud enough to lift the ceiling off the Euclid Avenue ice house.

This was the Barons' ninth Calder Cup championship in their history and the first since the 1957 campaign.

The Barons had to come from behind last night to clinch the triumph—as they have done so many times this year. The Aces scored at 1:26 of the first period on a pretty shot by their brilliant winger, Wayne Hicks.

The Aces seemed to have the upper hand for most of the first period. But after intermission, Coach Fred Glover's stalwarts stepped up the pace.

Len Ronson scored his first goal as a Baron at 10:49. Then the greatest of them all, Glover, scored at 18:07 to make it 2-1,

Cleveland, at the end of two periods.

The third line of center Cecil Hoekstra and wingers Guy Rousseau and Bob Ellet took charge the third period. Rousseau hit at 1:35 to make it 3-1. Jim Morrison, Quebec's strong defenseman, fired a 20-footer at 12:37 to make it 3-2 and throw a scare into the customers.

Cleveland has been known for strong hockey teams down through the years, but there never has been an assemblage such as this one wearing the blue shirts. Man-for-man, it's not the greatest in the AHL, but the way General Manager Jack Gordon and Glover put them together, it certainly has to rank as one of the league's finest fighting teams.

Glover went into the contest tied with Willie Marshall of Providence with 98 career playoff points. When Fred canned his goal in the second period it gave him sole possession of the mark with 47 goals and 52 assists for a 99-point record.

While Worsley again was outstanding in the Quebec goal, as he had been all season, Jean-Guy Morissette in the Cleveland end was equally as brilliant. Jean-Guy turned back several hard blasts that were sparklers. However, the little Frenchman also must consider himself a pretty lucky fellow.

Late in the second period, with the score tied at 1-1, Don Blackburn of Quebec came sailing in alone on Jean-Guy. He had the left side of the cage open, but his hard shot hit the post, glanced off the opposite post and bounced harmlessly away.

# Browns Smash Colts for NFL

# Championship

## by BOB AUGUST

### 12/64

In the third quarter yesterday, Johnny Unitas threw a short pass to fullback Jerry Hill as he angled toward the sideline. Browns linebacker Galen Fiss was approximately 10 yards away when Hill caught the ball.

Fiss closed the distance with a couple of strides and a headlong dive. What followed wasn't, in strictest terminology, a tackle. Legally, it could have been introduced in court as aggravated assault and battery, with intent to do great bodily harm. Fiss didn't wrap his arms around Hill. He merely collided with him, like a flying object, sending Hill back in the direction he had come from, flat on the trousers. The gain was two yards, and the Colt fullback paid in pain for each one.

The place to start in analyzing the Browns' amazing 27-0 victory is what they did to the Colts physically, like Fiss' tackle.

Naturally, strategy entered into it, things that can be demonstrated later on the blackboard with little x's and o's. But it wouldn't have made much difference without the muscle on the day the Browns' defense collectively played the game of its life.

When the deed had been accomplished, the Browns' dressing quarters settled down into the chaos standard to the crowning of a football champion. A crush of reporters bore in and the players, wearing happy smiles and not much else, explained how it happened. Photographers shouted for one more picture.

Picking his way through the jam, as he had once

Blanton Collier huddles with reporters following the stunning victory over the Colts.

maneuvered through a broken field, came chunky Buddy Young, former ball-carrying ace who now works for the Colts. "They told us this was a lousy team," said Young. "And they sure told us wrong."

This had been the story that was told about the Browns, passed surreptitiously around the league. According to the gossip they weren't the material from which champs are made, and the team's defense always took the knocks.

It had given up more yardage than any other in the National League. It was charged with being lucky to have survived.

When the game was over yesterday, the Browns' defense had no need to embrace Dame Fortune. It accomplished a shutout, a pro football rarity, against an outstanding offensive team, and it did it on merit.

The rush on Unitas was unrelenting, and the pass coverage quick and tight. In the first half, Unitas frequently darted out of trouble as his pocket collapsed on him. In the second half, the Browns closed this avenue of escape. Unitas' final passing yardage was a miserly 95 yards on one of the unhappiest days of his career.

There was nothing surprising about the Browns' offensive fireworks. Long delayed, they went off with a colorful burst in the third quarter. But the Browns are a team that can erupt this way.

Lou Groza set it off with his 43-yard field goal. Then the scores came fast. A 46-yard run by Jim Brown and a superb 18-yard touchdown pass from Frank Ryan to Gary Collins. Another touchdown pass covering 42 yards to a solitary Collins and, in a little over five minutes, the Browns had gone ahead, 17-0, and were counting their money.

In the fourth quarter, Groza's 10-yard field goal and Collins' third touchdown catch were merely decorative, but Collins' effort was highly fancy trimming. Ryan, passing into the strong wind, got the ball off high and far and Collins muscled it away from defender Bob Boyd for a 51-yard score.

When the mob reached the field and the goal-posts were falling, Ryan got a shoulder-high ride off the field. It was sweet retribution for the quarterback. In mid-season, some fans were suggesting he should get transportation out of town on a rail.

But if it was a great moment for Ryan, the triumphant point of his career, it was sweeter still for the defensive unit. The 27-0 shutout is in the record book for all time.

# Reflections on the Browns

## by JIM BROWN with STEVE DELSOHN

I look back on my career in pro football much the way a fan views the athletes and teams he cheered as a child: I prefer to recall the triumphs and good times, banish the disappointments to regions of my brain where they can't disturb me. I am fifty-three years old. Today when I think of Paul Brown, I remember the good times.

In a certain sense, Paul and I will always be married. We'll always be linked to each other, the history of the Cleveland Browns, and the history of the NFL. We had clashes, but they can't diminish our shared accomplishments. Not for me.

Dealing with a sports legend did get complicated. In Paul's case that isn't hyperbolic. To the public, Paul "was" the Cleveland Browns. Paul formed the team. He gave the Browns its name, his name, the Browns being the only NFL team ever named for their coach. For seventeen years Paul was the Browns' head coach and general manager, for most of that period one of its owners. In 1950 the Browns, San Francisco 49ers and Baltimore Colts were absorbed by the NFL. The cocky NFL thought the trio from the AAFC would be outclassed. Paul won the whole damn thing his first year. The Browns won Eastern Division titles the next five seasons, and two more NFL championships. Cleveland faltered when Otto Graham retired, revived when I appeared one year later. The bridge from past to present was Paul.

Paul literally invented much of modern coaching. Among his innovations: studying games on film, weekly grading of players from those films, utilizing playbooks, IQ tests for athletes. Paul started calling the plays for Otto Graham in 1946. Now it's standard. As players or assistants, Paul taught Don Shula, Chuck Knoll, Weeb Ewbank and Bill Walsh. They've

71

The greatest of them all, Jim Brown

coached ten Super Bowl winners.

Paul was a contained, chilly, brilliant, fanatically organized man, who once taught high school English. At the first team meeting every season, Paul would give his trademark speech: "You are a member of the Cleveland Browns. You are the New York Yankees of football. You will conduct yourself in a proper manner. I expect you to watch your language, your dress, your deportment. If you're a drinker or a chaser, you weaken the team and we don't want you. We're here for one thing—to win the championship. Let's get to work."

. . . His trademark as a coach was fear. He was a small, omnipotent man who could make people do things. Paul was all about performance and winning and organization, and Paul. He never spoke loudly because he didn't have to. He could reduce you with The Look, and a cutting one-liner.

Paul was famous for his one-liners. We used to have a chubby, jolly, left-handed halfback named Charley Scales. In a game against the Steelers our quarterback fumbled. Trying to salvage the play, Charles picked up the ball, decided he would throw me this little lefty pass. I was prepared—improvisation was one of my strong points—but Charley wobbled it, the pass was intercepted. As Charley ran off the field, Paul one-lined him: "you'll never have a chance to throw another one." True enough, Paul got rid of Charley a short time later.

. . . It wasn't a physical matter, that's never why football coaches frighten their athletes. It's Power—to play you, bench you, trade you, keep you. On the Browns the Power was Paul's. Though he hired some excellent assistants, allowed them their say, there was no doubt the man had given his style of ruling some thought. At team meetings we each had our own chair with our name tags taped to the back. If a guy's tag was showing Paul knew he was late. The guy would come sheepishly in, Paul would say nothing, everyone knew that man was fined fifty bucks. No questions asked, no wasted seconds. Paul was that organized.

I didn't mind all the rules. In one important way I liked

them. In the 1950's there was widespread racism, in the nation and in professional football. Paul's dictatorship discouraged cliques, and that discouraged racial prejudice. His rules were not to be questioned by anyone. We all had to abide by them equally. That was very pleasing to me.

The players made light of Paul's stiff ways but we also recognized his talent. Paul was the first NFL coach to administer tests to his athletes. At the onset of camp he would hand out written exams, long and impossibly hard. If you played offense, the play was a sweep, you had to know what you did, as well as the tackle, flanker, quarterback, every position. . . Lou Groza had been there seventeen years and was still taking the test, though his offensive tackle days were long over. Lou was just the kicker.

We'd laugh about those tests, never take them seriously, but we knew Paul wasn't crazy. Crazy? Man was smart. We cheated on those tests. Eighty degrees out in Palo Alto, guys were wearing long-sleeve shirts and sweaters. Had to hide those crib sheets. But after years of cheating, laughing at ourselves and at Paul, we drew a conclusion: Paul knew we were cheating. And didn't care. He knew in the process of cribbing, writing our plays on our sheets, we'd learn more than we would have otherwise. We said, "Damn, this guy is brilliant."

At the beginning, I loved playing for Paul. I was a runner. Paul wanted me to have the ball. I loved him for that. It was that simple.

Paul also planted a very nice one-liner on me that's now part of football lore. When people said Paul was working me too heavily, Paul didn't hesitate. He said, "When you've got a big gun, why not fire it as often as possible?" How can I "not" like a guy who says that?

I never wanted to be traded. Being a Cleveland Brown was more important to me than going to another town and making more money. I didn't sit around and wonder, What if I played for this team or that team. People said to me, "Man, if you played behind that line in Green Bay, behind Kramer and Thurston, you'd gain more yards." I never quite believed that. I had Ray Renfro and Paul Warfield and Gary Collins, receivers who would run downfield, block their butts off. I had Dick Shafrath, a lineman who would block at the line of scrimmage, hustle downfield and look for someone else. Gene Hickerson would work with me. John Wooten would work with me. And they'd work together: Hickerson and Wooten were one of the finest pulling guard tandems in NFL history. We didn't have the most talented line in football, but what we had was important: a perfect blend. I never wanted to leave that. I respected Jerry Kramer and Fuzzy Thurston, had no desire to play in Green Bay.

. . . I was Cleveland's first choice in the 1957 draft. Chosen before me were Lenny Dawson, Ron Kramer, John Brodie, Jon Arnett, and Paul Hornung. The week before camp, I'd been in Evanston, Illinois, at the college all-star game, where Otto Graham told me I'd never make it in the NFL. Later that week, in the game against the New York Giants, Curly Lambeau left me sitting on the bench. And I thought I was going to start! The only action I got was kicking off, and catching a couple passes late in the game. I was humiliated. After the game I left Soldiers Field, drove all night long to Hiram, Ohio, where the Browns had camp. I was the first rookie in camp, and I couldn't wait to begin pro ball.

Paul was equally anxious to get me started: our second exhibition game, he started me at fullback. We were in Akron, against the Pittsburgh Steelers, in the Rubber Bowl. Third quarter, I drove into the secondary, guys didn't know my speed, took the wrong angle, I broke a forty-yard TD. Paul pulled me out of the game. As I ran over the sideline, Paul called me over.

Paul said, "You're my fullback."

Then he walked away. I started grinning like a goddam clown. It was a huge moment. This guy was businesslike, his organization was tight, and he wanted to "use" me. I was never satisfied with my career at Syracuse. Though I'd overcome many things, "my" thing is constant performance, from day one to the end of the line. I wasn't allowed that at Syracuse, and it gnawed at me. Coming to Cleveland, Paul Brown, I felt like I'd died and gone to football heaven. I've never told anyone this, but when Paul said I was his fullback, it was the greatest moment I ever had in pro football.

. . . When Paul left Cleveland he was hurt and angry. And he bounced back. In 1970 he created the Cincinnati Bengals. Already, Paul has taken them twice to the Super Bowl. Paul is a force.

So is Art Modell. In their awe of Paul, a lot of folks failed to see that. Art understood business and money, had the ego to take on Paul Brown. When Art came to Cleveland, he was after three things: to create the TV doubleheader, bring a dose of Manhattan to the NFL, and rule the Cleveland Browns. He accomplished all three.

When Paul left the Browns my emotions ran the gamut. The image of him leaving, actually cleaning out his office, was disturbing. But I couldn't help but be pleased for Paul's successor, Blanton Collier. Blanton was the kind of man who makes you wonder how God decides who should die young and who should live to old age. When Blanton passed away it saddened the entire organization. He was a sweetheart of a human being.

As a coach Blanton was quiet, emotional, actually hugged a few guys as they ran the sideline. The players loved him, knew they were fortunate to have him: Blanton had been one of Paul's assistants. Out of loyalty to Paul, Blanton almost told Art no, refused the job.

For myself, I felt invigorated when we made the change. I had a need for self-expression. When Blanton came in I saw a chance to fulfill it again. I also knew the football world would be watching me. Not only because we'd stuck out our necks, complained about the offense. A lot of people believe that a runner can only excel in one system. Without Paul, there was some question as to how effective I might be. When I showed up at camp, I could run ninety yards without breathing hard. I "always" took pains to be in excellent shape, that was my thing, but this was a higher peak. I wanted to run the football the way no one had ever run it.

Blanton brought in Dub Jones, a former star receiver with the Browns, to help revamp the offense. Dub and Blanton were big hits with the guys on offense. They would consult us, listen to us, let us participate in devising plays. Blanton started running me around the ends. He let me catch passes. I even threw some, and if you don't think that was a blast, then you've never played running back. Blanton worked closely with our quarterback, Frank Ryan. And Frank began to emerge as a passer. Frank had always been long on brains and courage, but he'd been dealt a rough hand. We were a running team, I dominated the press, Frank was always overlooked. Wounded pride can hurt, not as much as a broken body: under Paul, when Frank threw at all, it was often third and long, and Frank got roughed up. I never wanted to give the ball, say, Here man, you be the meat of the offense. Yet I felt for him. On another team, I knew he'd be more appreciated.

Blanton also instituted an option play. The offensive linemen would take their men wherever they wanted to. I would read their blocks, and go. I had good peripheral vision, I could pick, and this was ideal for me. Though we only had one option play, and as up man in the I formation, I didn't have a lot of room to play with, the option was a godsend. It was instinctual football and I averaged about nine yards on that sucker. And if I'd had that option play from day one, my career might have been unbelievable.

As it was, for the first time in years, I was free to roam the entire field and to use all the skills I brought to the game. It was a good year (1963). Though the Giants won the division at 11-3, we went 10-4, split our series with them, and had some fun. Liberated by Blanton, with my boys on the line doing some blasting, I was a running fool. I had rushed for 1,863 yards, averaged 6.3 yards a carry. Had games of 162, 232, 175, 123, 144, 223, 154, 179, and 125. I was twenty-seven years old. I never ran better in my life.

In 1964, we played the Baltimore Colts for the NFL championship. We'd been beaten by the Giants twice, finished 10-3-1, but the Colts were stacked, had gone 12-2. Supposedly, they were going to whip us. We beat them 27-0. I played well, Frank Ryan threw three TDs to Gary Collins, who won the game MVP. And the defense was magnificent. To shut out Johnny Unitas and Ray Berry and Lenny Moore, anytime, was almost inconceivable. To do it in a game that big "was" inconceivable. We had a tough undersized linebacker named Vince Costello, who'd been there ever since I had, and Vince kicked some ass. Also fantastic was Bernie Parrish. Bernie and the rest of our defensive backs did something revolutionary for 1964: they moved up to the line of scrimmage, started popping Baltimore's receivers. It screwed up Baltimore's timing, played a large role in our victory.

I've always loved how that game unfolded. Team Victory is an overworked phrase, but this was it. I knew there were guys on the team who must have felt slighted all those years, watching the reporters always question me, and if they did question them, it was often for a quote about me. It wasn't the way it is today, with 90 million reporters for every player. But after we beat the Colts, reporters were bouncing from guy to guy, and those guys were "yapping." I knew they could take that feeling home, have a championship in their life, no matter what happened after that day.

My first NFL championship. . . I felt potent. Sentimental. Grateful. Whole. . . I also felt intense relief. Unless he wins a championship, even a superstar is never fully accepted. Some people use the absence of a title to criticize a successful individual. They say a team "can't" win a championship with him. He's too much of a soloist. Otto Graham announced it to the world about me.

So it felt GOOD to get that primate off my back. I said, Self, breathe this in, and don't be in any rush. You got exactly where you wanted to go. In life that is rare.

So is repeating and we couldn't pull it off. We went all the way back to the title game, but Lombardi's Packers denied us, 23-12. Those guys were roughed and skilled, but I think they received an assist from the elements. The game was in Green Bay, the field was ice, and we couldn't run. They'll hate me for this: I think we would have won in normal conditions.

I retired after that season, and I retired happy. Those last three years were a romp.

A typically frustrated Bill Fitch, Cavalier Head Coach

# The Bad Old Days, Early Cavs

## by DAN COUGHLIN

We sat around the lunch table Monday—which is what traveling sportswriters do before they sit down for dinner—and prodded the story of the Cavaliers' genesis from two men who were there at the beginning—Bill Nichols and Joe Tait.

When Nichols inherited the job of pro basketball writer for *The Plain Dealer*, nobody lined up to offer congratulations. I didn't know whether to send flowers or a Mass Card.

"That first year nobody second-guessed what I wrote," Nichols recalled, "because nobody read it."

Tait recalled that he almost quit 12 hours after accepting the job as the radio voice of the basketball team.

Actually, Tait wasn't aboard for the team's maiden voyage. He was hired several games into the first season in October, 1970. Bob Brown, assistant to Cavs' founder Nick Mileti, broadcast the first several games while Mileti pondered which route to take.

"He didn't know whether to go to New York and get a big-time broadcaster, or bring one in from the sticks," Tait said as he chewed on a char-broiled cheeseburger. "After a few games Nick knew it would be disastrous to hire a big timer. The team was so bad the guy probably would quit after three weeks or he'd knock the team so bad they would have wished he would quit."

Cavs' coach Bill Fitch told Mileti he knew a sportscaster in Terre Haute, Indiana, who was so dumb he probably would take the job. Mileti couldn't believe anybody was that dumb and he wanted to meet him.

"I had given up sportscasting by then," Tait said. "I was the general manager of a station in Terre Haute. I wasn't going to beat the bushes all my life and wind up a broken down sportscaster in a small town at the age of 50.

"I had known Bill Fitch when he was coaching at Coe College and I was broadcasting at Monmouth College. We had the worst team in the conference. When he got the Cleveland job, I wrote him a letter of congratulations. My application for the broadcasting job was a PS at the end of the letter. 'Do you want me to do the same thing for you that I did at Monmouth College?' I said.

"When Bill talked to me he warned me that the Cavaliers were a bad team. 'As bad as Monmouth?' I said. 'Worse,' he said."

So Tait came to Cleveland to meet Mileti, who told him to broadcast a game into a tape recorder. That night Mileti listened to the tape and the next morning at 9 a.m. he called him and offered him the job. As dumb as Tait was, he even made the Cavaliers sound exciting. Mileti liked that. So did thousands of listeners, it turned out.

"I went home to Terre Haute that night to pack my bags and I listened to Andy Musser broadcast the 76ers-Cavs game from Philadelphia. I almost backed out of the deal that night," said Tait.

That was the game the Cavaliers, who were still winless, lost by 54 points. Afterward, Fitch fined every player $54.

During his broadcast, Musser sounded awed by the Cavs' ineptitude.

"This team is so bad it won't win a game this season," Musser said. "The Cavaliers aren't good enough to play in the Eastern League. They're the worst team I've ever seen. When the Cleveland fans see how bad they are, they won't come to the games and the team will go broke. I don't know how they'll last the season. This might be the only time we'll ever see this team."

Tait said he was serious. He almost called the whole thing off.

"But Nick figured I'd be impressed by the big city, the tall buildings, the airplanes and the hotels—and he was right," said

Tait.

I met Tait for the first time several games later in San Francisco, where that night the Cavs lost their 15th straight game, setting a record at the time for NBA masochism. Late in the game during a time out, Bingo Smith urged his team to rally. "Let's go, we're only down by 10," said Smith. Fitch looked up at the scoreboard which said Warriors 96, Cavaliers 66, and he knew math was not Smith's forte.

That was the night a security guard refused to let Fitch in the auditorium because he didn't have a ticket. The guard relented because he said nobody would admit to being the coach of the Cavaliers unless he really was.

That night Fitch, Tait and I walked back to the hotel through a wet San Francisco fog and Fitch stopped to berate a fire hydrant. Fitch was seething. "Johnny Egan couldn't guard that fireplug," he said.

The next night in Portland the Cavs won their first game by one point, but they weren't sure the game was over because the buzzer failed to work. Tait had to ask into a live microphone. "Did we win?" It was the first of only 15 games the Cavs won that first season of 1970-71.

A few weeks later the Cavs beat Philadelphia and Andy Musser, who was in Minneapolis on a football assignment, spilled a beer all over himself when he saw the score on the television.

The next year when Stretch Howard refused to tape a halftime interview with Tait, Rick Roberson grabbed him and ordered him to do the interview. Roberson pointed at Tait. "He's the only man who says anything nice about us," said Roberson.

Those were the things we talked about while awaiting the showdown Monday night with the Washington Bullets. We had to keep reminding ourselves that yesterday's nightmare and today's dream world are all part of the same story.

Bruce Crampton congratulates the 1973 PGA Champion, Jack Nicklaus.

# Nicklaus Wins PGA and Record

# 14th Major

## by BILL NICHOLS
## 8/73

Jack Nicklaus now stands alone in the glorious history of golf.

Nicklaus, the famed Golden Bear, easily won the PGA National Championship at Canterbury Golf Club yesterday to become the all-time leader on the list of winners of the prestigious major titles.

The PGA is Nicklaus' 14th major championship, one more than was recorded by the late Bobby Jones, a legendary golf figure of another era.

He topped runner-up Bruce Crampton by four strokes to equal the widest margin of victory in the championship since it changed to stroke play in 1958. Al Geiberger set the four-shot margin record when he won the PGA at Firestone in 1966.

Nicklaus picked up the winner's check for $45,000 to boost his 1973 earnings to $245,424, placing him second to Crampton on the money list.

Crampton pocketed $25,700 and now has banked $270,841 this year.

Crampton checked in with a final round 33-37—70 for a 72-hole total of three-under-par 281.

Another shot in arrears were Lanny Wadkins (69), J. C. Snead (69) and Mason Rudolph (73). At one-under regulation were Tom Weiskopf (71) and Don Iverson (74). At even par were Hale Irwin, Kermit Zarley and 61-year-old Sam Snead.

There were challenges, but no one was able to do so seriously. Nicklaus was determined to win this championship and there was little doubt that he would at anytime yesterday afternoon.

Jack held a one-shot lead on Rudolph and Iverson when the final round got underway. The Bear would not falter.

Nicklaus contented himself with par through the first five holes and then birdied Nos. 6 and 7 for an outgoing 34. On the home nine he filed in a 22-foot putt on 15 for a bird and finished with his only three-putt effort for the tournament on the 18th for a bogey.

Interestingly, Nicklaus had just five bogies in 72 holes in the last four days.

"I am absolutely delighted," he said afterwards.

"Obviously, I've been bugged this year. Everytime (in major championships) I've fouled up a round when I had a chance to win.

"I played just solid golf," he added, "nothing sensational, but just solid and I feel I putted pretty well on these greens."

The turning point in the tournament, Nicklaus said, was his second shot on the 465-yard 13th hole. He had used a three wood off the tee instead of a driver for accuracy but nevertheless had pushed the ball into the right rough.

A tree obscured his view of the green. He hooked a four iron around around the tree and rolled the ball onto the front green 30 feet from the pin. He two putted for par and maintained his three-stroke lead.

Crampton, who finished second to Nicklaus at both the 1972 U. S. Open and Masters, had nothing but praise for the champion.

"This borders on the unbelievable," said Bruce. "Playing along Jack was wonderful for me. It was an honor to be an eyewitness to history. It's incredible for a man to accomplish so much and be so young."

Crampton began the day at two-under par and made a charge on the front nine with a 33. He stumbled just enough o lose his challenging position on the back and was content to receive the runner-up check.

Crampton, however, needed help to finish second. Rudolph supplied it when he came apart on the 18th and 72nd hole with a double bogey six to finish in a tie for third.

Rudolph struggled in with a closing 73 and 282 total.

Rudolph and Iverson trailed Nicklaus by one swing after 54 holes. Iverson closed with a 74 and he finished in a tie for sixth worth $7,311.

. . . Someone asked Nicklaus about comparing himself with Jones and he said it can't be done. "That was a different time; there was different competition and different golf courses," he said.

"You can't even draw any comparisons until I retire and I'm not about to retire. I plan to play a lot more golf."

What about winning his 14th major. "Fourteen is just a number," said Jack. "You have to wait for history to list the records."

Nicklaus failed to win Number 14 in his last five major championships, which caused someone to remark, "Didn't you believe it would happen someday?" With that, Jack replied, "I never believe things will happen. You have to make it happen."

It happened Sunday at Canterbury. He became a legend in his own time.

How did he feel? "I don't know," he answered. "It will take a few days for the impact to sink in."

John Lowenstein greets a jubilant Frank Robinson after Robby's historic home run.

# Frank Robinson's Amazing

# Managerial Debut

## by RUSSELL J. SCHNEIDER
## 4/75

Cleveland, Ohio, Apr. 8—Cleveland Municipal Stadium did not collapse in a heap of rubble when manager Frank Robinson carried his first lineup card to the plate and handed it to umpire Nestor Chylak. The Stadium did shudder ever so perceptibly under the thunderous cheers of 56,715 baseball fans when player Frank Robinson smashed a home run in his very first time at bat. It was, without a doubt, one of the most dramatic moments in baseball. As the ball arched higher and deeper to left center field, the fans stood as one, roaring approval. The Yankee pitcher, Doc Medich, reached for another ball, trying to shrug off the ramifications of what had just happened.

"It gave me goose bumps and it took all the pressure off the rest of us," said Boog Powell, who homered later in the game, ensuring the Indians' 5-3 victory.

Thrilled, too, was winning pitcher Gaylord Perry, who was the first to leap out of the Indians' dugout to greet Robinson after his home run. And when the game ended with another standing ovation, Robinson was the first to greet Perry coming off the field. Both times the men embraced: the white, Southern-born pitcher and the black manager.

"Any home run is a thrill, but I've got to admit this one was a bigger thrill," confessed Robinson, whose office was packed with writers, broadcasters, and cameramen after the dramatic debut.

For the record, Robinson delivered with the count at 2 and

2, on the eighth pitch by Medich. The first two were quick strikes. Robinson fouled off the next two, two more were wide, then another foul, all preceding the homer. When Robinson reached the plate and before he was mobbed by his players, he doffed his cap. "That was for my wife." Barbara was seated with son Kevin and daughter Nichelle in the loges behind the plate.

The homer made general manager Phil Seghi, the man who hired Robinson, something of a prophet.

"Phil suggested to me this morning, 'Why don't you hit a homer the first time you go to the plate?'" related Robinson. "I told him, 'You've got to be kidding.'"

Later, Seghi said, "I might have suggested he hit a homer, but I never dreamed he'd do it. I should have. Knowing Frank, I shouldn't be surprised by anything about the man's ability to rise to an occasion. Frank Robinson doing the unusual is only usual for him."

Robinson admitted he could hardly believe what happened as he toured the bases to the cheering of the crowd.

"At first there was nothing running through my mind really," he said. "But by the time I got to third base, I thought to myself, Wow, will miracles never cease?"

It was, Robinson said, "The single most satisfying thing that happened, other than winning. Right now I feel better than I have after anything I've done in baseball. Take all the pennants, the personal awards, the World Series, the All-Star games, and this moment is the greatest."

He also spoke of the crowd. "It was unbelievable. If I could have asked God for a good day, I never would have asked for something like this and expected it to happen. Everything was all I could ask for."

It was almost all Rachel Robinson could ask for, too. Jackie Robinson's widow was invited by the Indians to throw out the ceremonial first pitch. In her pregame remarks, Rachel Robinson said, "I want to say I'm proud to be here, and I want to congratulate you for honoring yourselves by being the first to take this historic step." And later, "I've wished, since I was asked to do this, that Jackie could be here, and I'm sure in many ways he is."

Mrs. Robinson continued, saying she was "heartened by this symbol of progress," but said Jackie had always hoped it would happen sooner. "I hope this is the beginning of a lot more black players being moved into the front office and managerial positions and not just having their talents exploited on the field."

When asked if Frank Robinson's success—or failure—as a manager might have any bearing on the hiring of other blacks as managers, Rachel Robinson replied softly, but with some defiance, "Why should it? White men have failed as managers, but it has not harmed the chances of other white men."

Barbara Robinson, when introduced at a luncheon, stood alongside Rachel Robinson and delivered a short and simple speech. "If it were not for Rachel and Jackie, I would not be here today."

Bowie Kuhn also spoke during the pregame ceremonies. "This is an historic day in baseball and I am happy on behalf of baseball to bring its greetings to Frank Robinson and the Cleveland Indians . . . to bring our congratulations to the management of the Cleveland Indians Baseball Club. We hope you have a great season in Cleveland."

Yankee manager Bill Virdon came up with the best postgame remark. Smiling and pleasant despite the defeat, Virdon observed wryly, "Well, I guess this makes me the answer to one of those trivia questions. Who was the losing manager the day a black man managed for the first time in the big leagues?"

Seghi, beaming with pride, proclaimed, "There wasn't one single disappointment for me, not one. It was the kind of day, the kind of a game you only dream about, like Alice in Wonderland."

Dick Snyder's miracle shot

# Miracle in Richfield

## by HAL LEBOVITZ
### 4/76

How do write about it? Where are the adjectives?

Incredible . . . stupendous . . . overwhelming . . . a miracle . . .

Those words are all too tame.

The noise hasn't stopped. These ears will ring forever.

They're still tearing up the Coliseum as these words are being written. Fans are going absolutely ape . . . The baskets have been torn down . . . These mad, mad fans . . . Deliriously mad.

Are you beginning to get the picture?

The hero, Dick Snyder, had to run up into the stands to get into the locker room. Otherwise he would have been killed—with love.

It was Snyder's drive-in basket in the last four seconds that put this never-to-be-forgotten playoff series against the Bullets to an end. The final score? Who remembers? Who cares? The Cavs won by two points. The scoreboard says 87-85. It must be right.

How much closer can a series get? This never-to-be-forgotten match between these two hungry, tenacious fighting teams came down to those last four seconds. Either team could have won.

The Cavs did because they refused to buckle under a fantastic shooting performance by Phil Chenier. It was Snyder who had the burden of guarding him. It was the Bullets' simple strategy to isolate the brilliant shooter against Snyder. They had learned in previous games that Dave Bing's offensive threat had been nullified by Jim Cleamons. Big Nate Thurmond could do a number on Elvin Hayes when necessary.

But nobody could stop Chenier. It had been proved in the

93

previous game.

It took a whole team to beat Chenier—all the Cavs. Except for a slight letdown in the second period, they moved constantly. They never stopped trying. It paid off—at the very end.

Snyder was the epitome of this hustle. He could have hung his head. Chenier kept dropping those beauties, no matter how close Snyder played him. It seemed futile. But Dick kept at it. He caused a couple of turnovers; he saved some balls from going out of bounds. And, as it says in the good book, if you never quit, if you keep on trying, something good eventually will happen. It did. Finally, in the last few seconds.

It's not right to single out heroes on this TEAM. Snyder's basket won it. But the board work provided the ultimate victory. That takes a TEAM.

There are clubs as tough as the Bullets under the boards. Big Wes Unseld is a mountain under there. Hayes is exceptional. Yet Nate Thurmond and Jim Brewer beat them on the boards. The little guys helped them, too. The Cavs won because they turned their rebounds into baskets. They got some second shots. And when Chenier missed they didn't give the Bullets any.

The Bullets, of course, are sick. They played their hearts out, too. Their defense was exceptional. The Cavs seldom got a clear shot. They had to force them with fine fakes and drives. Jim Cleamons gets a gold star for his determination in going to the hoop. Eventually his shots, tough, hard fought shots, began to fall in. It's too bad anybody had to lose. But the Cavs won . . . and it was no fluke.

If there was a turning point in this torrid game it had to be the fifth foul committed by Chenier, a foolish grabbing one. He had to sit awhile and play a little more cautiously when he returned. It cooled him somewhat. But what cooled him even more was Nate Thurmond's switches. Thurmond turned this team into a real winner when he arrived. And he could help them go all the way.

All the way?

More of the same? How much can one heart take? How much can human eardrums take?

The Coliseum has been turned into a boiler factory for these playoff games. Constant pounding. Wall-to-wall noise.

And now the Cavs go on to meet either the Boston Celtics or the Buffalo Braves.

You say those games will be anti-climactic? Nothing could top the series just past? Don't bet on it. With these Cavs scrapping and these fans screaming it's possible the crescendo has yet to be reached. If a mere human body can take it.

Before the game the Cavs came out of the locker room, after they met with their exceptional coach, Bill Fitch, and held their own little meeting in the tunnel. They held hands. "Let's play it cool. Let's play it together," said Thurmond.

They played it cooler than the fans. But the fans played it together—all 21,564 of them. In the final three minutes it was impossible to hear the whistle, or the buzzer. It was impossible to see unless you stood.

So now what do the fans and the Cavs do for an encore? If they do nothing more, they've already done it. But if the building is still standing they may even top themselves.

. . . And the beat goes on.

Airport welcome for the Kardiac Kids after clinching division title

# The Kardiac Kids

## by BOB SUDYK
## 12/80

It was eerie, almost ghostlike and certainly a dream in the blue-white kleig lights which greeted the Central Division championship Browns at Hopkins Airport last night. Thousands of fans cheered themselves hoarse, with hearts so warm, the chill was taken from the cold night air, which hovered around 10 degrees.

The Browns . . . champions of the best division in professional football, dethroning the Pittsburgh Steelers' dynasty?

Did it really happen?

The airport scene held the imagination of a Fellini movie. Players stepping across a makeshift stage with their coaches. Mayor George Voinovich hugging and kissing Browns' owner Art Modell.

Screaming fans leaving clouds of vapor in the air. "The Twelve Days of a Browns Christmas" being sung and chanted. Coach Sam Rutigliano smiling shyly, waving somewhat subdued, as if in vague fear too much emotion might pop the bubble. That he might suddenly awake, and find himself in bed in the first July morning of the 1980 workouts.

Let the players say what they want. Let the coaching staff tell you how this team pulled off the biggest miracle here since the 1948 World Champion baseball team. Let them tell you they knew it all along. I dare them.

One of the giant surprises, defensive end Marshall Harris, yanked off his 10-gallon cowboy hat and pitched it to the crowd behind the fence. Defensive back Clarence Scott, unable to bridle his emotions, exploded in a soul-disco solo.

97

Calvin Hill passed out victory cigars. Modell broke open champagne on the flight home. Tackle Doug Dieken explained there wasn't any wild champagne celebration in the locker room because, "We're not a bunch of out-of-shape degenerates like baseball players."

Instead, Rutigliano led his players in a team prayer of thanksgiving for the riches bestowed upon them.

Nobody pretended to know all along this miracle was going to happen. Not until the final seven seconds, when Steve Kreider caught Ken Anderson's pass on the Browns' 14-yard line as time ran out, did the Browns actually become champs with a 27-24 victory over the highly-fueled Cincinnati Bengals.

Typically, the Browns' didn't take the field-goal lead until 75 seconds remained on the regular season clock.

Brian Sipe, in my book the finest quarterback machine in pro football, stood not far from me on the frigid turf. The gun sounded ending the game. He and the teammates near him froze for a moment. They turned to each other. Some turned to the scoreboard and clock to make certain.

It had happened.

They began leaping for the clouds, the ones numbered nine.

They hoisted Rutigliano on their shoulders and carried the heart and soul of their team upon their backs tenderly being careful not to hurt the man who put this all together. Those of us who criticize him for losing occasional battles must heap laurels upon the man who won the war.

Whatever chemistry that exists which produces a second-guess on his strategy is the same chemistry which made a winner of a team that is not the most talented in the game.

Rutigliano suggested that the club spend some time on the "Carry the Coach off the Field Drill." He quipped, "Weeb Ewbank suffered a dislocated hip on one of those rides. Each guy had one of my legs, I thought they were going to make a wish."

He added thoughtfully, "There is tremendous emotion in this locker room. This is a team of a lot little great people, from

Brian Sipe to Dino Hall. We had no stars. Sipe took a fairly good team and an average coach and won a title."

Sipe, boyish and enthusiastic for life itself, recalled that final moment on the field. "I was numb. I'm so accustomed to bad things happening over the years. We finally did it. I'm still in a state of shock."

Gulping for air in the crush of writers, Sipe said, "It's Sam. He turned my career around. He came with ideas and philosophy that makes so much sense. It's his strength of character which is transmitted to a team."

It is also transmitted to Modell who, at times during the stress of a game, appears to be suffering a gall bladder attack. Normally, owners intimidate their coaches. While this treatment is not to suggest Sam as the patron saint of the NFL, he has transmitted a calm to Modell, in my opinion.

This is not because two grown men kissed each other on the cheek yesterday.

Modell said of his miracle team, which has had 24 of its last 32 games decided in the last two minutes: "This is a helluva field organization. I think this team is an over-achiever. We don't have the depth of talent other teams have. But it has an intangible, an instinct for victory."

I believe the Browns got this far because they were very fortunate in suffering no serious injuries to key people. But winning so many hair-raising victories is not luck.

Perhaps never before has the term, "team," really expressed the true meaning of the word more than Sam's bunch of boys in our town—a town that is somebody once again.

After a horrid exhibition season and two opening regular-season defeats, the Browns have won 11 of their last 14 games.

The Super Bowl? Why not? Such a dream holds more reality than anything anyone imagined the Browns would have accomplished three months ago.

Red Right 88

# Red Right 88

## by BILL LEVY
## 1/81

Cleveland's winter weather was about as bad as it could have been during the week preceding the showdown between the Browns and the Raiders. Heavy snows buried the tarpaulin covering the field and the turf was frozen solid. At midweek, snowplows equipped with rubber blades cleared the snow. Huge kerosene blowers were placed under the edges of the tarp and around the clock hot air was pumped in to thaw the field. The Browns worked out in the cold all week, but the Raiders took their time getting to Cleveland—and who could blame them? The Raiders arrived late Friday on a chartered 747, just slipping in under the NFL's mandatory rule that visiting teams must be at the site at least 36 hours before game time.

Sunday morning dawned bitterly cold. The temperature hovered near zero. Those with tickets had a choice. They could brave the elements or they could stay home and watch the game on television because it was a sell-out and the traditional blackout had been lifted. Only a few thousand decided to rough it in their family rooms. The rest, 77,000 persons, trundled off to Cleveland Stadium in the warmest wear they could find. Situated on the edge of Lake Erie, the Stadium is not a place for the fainthearted on wintery days, when lake winds lash in and swirl around the giant horseshoe. As they headed for the stadium on the streets of downtown Cleveland, the street merchants were out in force, selling Browns paraphernalia and souvenirs—t-shirts, signs, woolen hats, etc. Despite the devastating cold, the entire scene had a carnival-like atmosphere.

Inside the stadium, the field looked like an island surrounded by snow and tarps strewn around at random. Hundreds of hand-made signs were hung over the upper and lower deck railings: "On to the Siper Bowl." "Believe." "Nobody but Cleveland."

Heated benches for the players had been trucked in from Philadelphia overnight after they had been used the day before in the Philadelphia-Minnesota NFC showdown which the Eagles had won. The temperature at game time was one degree with a 35 below zero wind chill factor. The wind was blowing at 16 mph from the northwest. It was not a day fit for man or beast or football.

. . . With 2:40 remaining in the third period, Cockroft kicked his second field goal, a 29-yard shot, to give the Browns a 12-7 margin which was the score when the period ended.

As it had done at the end of the second quarter, the Oakland offense suddenly came to life. And in a drive which started on their own 20 on the last play of the third quarter and consumed nearly six minutes, the Raiders marched down the field. The tough running of King and Van Eeghen was masterfully combined with the passing of Plunkett, who completed passes of 19 yards to Cliff Branch and 27 yards to Chester. The Raiders had a first down and goal to go at the Cleveland three. Plunkett called on the durable Van Eeghen. He slugged ahead for two yards on the first try, then inched ahead to the one-foot line on the next. Finally, on third down he rolled over the goal line to put the Raiders out in front. Chris Bahr conversion made it 14-12.

With the clock showing 4:39 remaining, the Browns took over the ball on their own 28, after a short Guy punt. On the first play, Sipe was forced to scramble and fumbled and Oakland's Otis McKinley recovered at the Cleveland 25. There was a stunned silence in the beige horseshoe on the lake. The Raiders called on Van Eeghen once again. One yard to the 24, eight yards to the 16, another half-yard to the 15 1/2. Now it was fourth down and a half-yard to go for the first down. Coach Tom Flores decided against going for what would be a 32-yard field goal, and instead called for another Van Eeghen smash.

The 225-pound, 6'2" back hurled into the right side of the Cleveland line. It did not give an inch. The Browns had the ball. They were alive, 85 yards from their own goal line. The clock showed 2:22 remaining. There was plenty of time for another miracle finish, a patented Kardiac Kids charge that would swipe victory from the Raiders in the final seconds.

On first down, Sipe's pass to Rucker was too long. On second down, Sipe slipped on the slick turf but managed to connect with Newsome on the left side for 29-yard completion. The official signaled the two-minute warning and the Browns were on their own 45. The fans were on their feet yelling "Go, Go, Go."

Brian's pass to Greg Pruitt was incomplete and then the Browns quarterback lost a yard on a broken play. On a third down and 11 play, Dwayne O'Steen was called for interference on Reggie Rucker and Cleveland had first down on the Oakland 49. Sipe then fired to Greg Pruitt down the left side, the little running back caught it and dashed out of bounds at the Oakland 28. The clock showed 1:12 remaining. After an incomplete pass, Sipe handed off to Mike Pruitt and the former Purdue star exploded up the middle for a 14-yard gain, and a first down on the Oakland 14. Pruitt went up the middle again for another yard. The Browns called time out with little more than a half-minute remaining. Rutigliano huddled with Sipe and Jim Shofner on the sidelines. If the Browns failed to gain anything in the next two downs, they could still win with a field goal. But a field goal was no sure thing, even at that distance. Don Cockroft had kicked only 18 of 32 field goals during the season, and had already missed two on the frozen turf at the open end of the Stadium. He had also been affected by knee and sciatic nerve problems since early in the season and this obviously had affected his kicking. Sipe thought the Browns would run the ball for the next two plays and was shocked when Rutigliano, who had been criticized for gambling too frequently when the situation did not dictate, called "Red Right 88," a pass play. Sam also told Sipe: "If you get in trouble and the receivers are covered, throw the ball into Lake Erie." Sipe questioned the call initially, but then agreed with the strategy to try one pass, run on the next down and attempt the field goal. On the "Red Right 88" play, Dave Logan, on the left, was the intended receiver. He was to run under the coverage into the right corner while Ozzie Newsome and Reggie Rucker were to cross over.

Sipe returned to the field, took the snap and faded back quickly. He did not want to get sacked, taking the Browns out of field goal range. Logan cut toward the right corner, but weak safety Burgess Owens was there with him. Sipe opted to throw to Newsome who was cutting over the middle to the left side of the end zone. In the meantime, Owens had cut free of Logan, leaving him wide open, and moved in front of Newsome along with strong safety Mike Davis. Sipe's pass arched slightly behind Newsome. Davis lunged for the ball and intercepted with 49 seconds remaining. The Browns had run out of miracles. The Kardiac Kids were dead for this season.

Gambling Sam had rolled the dice for six and crapped. You could hear the collective groans of the Cleveland fans all the way to Oakland, California. The Cleveland Stadium turned into a giant, frigid mausoleum and most of the fans left their seats and headed for the exits.

Sipe, who was knocked to the turf as he unloaded the ball, did not see the end of the play. He heard the fans and he knew that the season was over. As he walked dejectedly to the sideline, he was greeted by Rutigliano. "I love you," Sam said reassuringly. "I love you." The Raiders ran out the clock to preserve the 14-12 victory, the first stop on the road to the Super Bowl, a 27-10 win over Philadelphia and the World Championship.

Rutigliano, a compulsive gambler on the sidelines, had no apology for the call. "We felt the field goal was no gut cinch," he said in the dressing room. "It was our plan to throw on second down, then run the ball on third down and if we didn't get it into the end zone by then, go for the field goal. The play we called was a play that has been successful in the past. Unfortunately, it was an errant throw. But I'd rather put my money in Sipe's arm than take a chance on a field goal."

Sipe admitted in the locker room that he had questioned the call. "But we've done so well playing that kind of offense. I thought we would run the ball, the staff was adamant it was the right play."

Oakland's Plunkett had perhaps the most thoughtful explanation for the decision by the Browns. "I believe the wind is the reason they didn't run the ball into position for a field goal try," he said. "It was tough at that end of the field and they had those problems earlier. Remember, all the points except for the Cleveland touchdown on the interception were scored on the closed end of the field."

Strangely enough, there were no tears in the Cleveland locker room. Perhaps Brian Sipe summed it up best: "I am not going to sing the blues because we lost," he said. "We lost, but it was too great a year to be singing the blues. We did things dramatically all season, and I guess it is only fitting that we lose in a dramatic fashion,"

"I am not going to let this get me down, or the team," he continued, surrounded by hordes of writers. "We've played a lot of good football. We won the AFC Central after nobody gave us a chance, and we played it right down to the wire. I'm disappointed, but I am going home to San Diego and be damned happy with what we accomplished."

"But the important thing," said Sipe, who completed only 13 of 40 passes to his frozen receivers for 182 yards and had three interceptions, "is that we had a dream—and we almost made it come true."

There had been many more productive seasons in the 34-year history of the Cleveland Browns, but considering the fact that the Browns had been out of the play-offs for so long, there certainly had never been a more satisfying season.

Len Barker is swarmed by the media and security following his perfect game.

# Barker's Perfect Game

## by BURT GRAEFF

### 5/81

No one ever before said that Large Lenny Barker was perfect. Today, it can be said: Large Lenny Barker was perfect.

Leonard Harold Barker, for 2 hours and 9 minutes last night at the Stadium, was as perfect as a pitcher of baseballs can be.

Twenty-seven times players wearing Toronto Blue Jays uniforms came to home plate. Twenty-seven times they returned to the third base dugout, each failing to get so far as first base.

The twenty-seventh hitter, Ernie Whitt, stroked a lazy fly ball towards center field at precisely 9:45 p.m.

Rick Manning, who threw his arms out in glee at the crack of the bat, camped under and snagged the fly ball.

Baseball history had been made in Cleveland.

Barker's 3-0 perfect-game no hitter is:

• The 11th in the history of the major leagues.

• The last occurred in 1968 when Jim (Catfish) Hunter of Oakland decisioned Minnesota, 4-0, on May 8.

• The second by an Indians pitcher. Adrian (Addie) Joss was perfect in a 1-0 victory over Chicago in a game here at Dunn Field.

• It was the 85th no-hitter in American League history, the 194th in major league history. The last American League no-hitter was pitched by Bert Blyleven, then of the Texas Rangers. Blyleven, now, with the Indians, no-hit the California Angels, Sept. 22, 1977.

• It was the 15th no-hitter by an Indians' pitcher, the first since May 30, 1977 when Dennis Eckersley blanked the California Angels, 1-0, at the Stadium.

Barker, now 3-1 on the season with a 1.06 earned-run-average, needed just 113 pitches to write himself into the record books. Eighty-four of them were strikes, 29 were balls.

The 25-year old Pennsylvanian, who once threw a wild pitch that nearly landed in the press box at Fenway Park in Boston, struck out 11. They were all swinging strike-outs and all came after the fourth inning. No batter had a 3-ball count and only eight had as much as a 2-ball count.

Pitching coach Dave Duncan sensed something special in the making as he watched Barker warm up in the right field bullpen prior to the game.

"He started out slow in his warm-ups," said Duncan. "But as he went along, his curve ball got better and better. It became awesome. It wasn't breaking much, but the rotation was so tight it was almost like the perfect curve ball.

Barker, along with catcher Ron Hassey, used that almost perfect curve ball almost exclusively as the game wore on. There were just 17 fast balls thrown after the fourth inning. Only 16 pitches after the fourth were called balls by home plate umpire Rich Garcia.

"I thought he (Barker) did a pretty good job," said Hassey, trying to keep a straight face.

"By the fifth inning, his breaking ball was going so good we figured that's what we'd stay with. By the time the ninth inning came, we decided that if there was going to be a base hit, it would have to come off a breaking pitch."

The Blue Jays, whose .218 batting average is the lowest in the American League, entered the game without scoring a run in their 21 previous innings. They had been shut out in the previous two games, both against Baltimore.

The 7,290 fans in attendance for this game, which began in a drizzle and the temperature at 49 degrees, were standing and chanting, "Len-nie, Len-nie" as early as the start of the eighth inning.

Rick Bosetti opened the inning by popping out to Toby Harrah on a 1-1 pitch. Al Woods, batting for Danny Ainge, then fanned on an 0-an-2 pitch.

The 27th batter Ernie Whitt, a 28-year old catcher who was sent up to bat for Buck Martinez, was next.

Whitt, batting .188, swung and missed the first pitch. He let the second go by for a ball. He swung and fouled off yet another Barker curve that nailed Hassey on the leg and trickled down the first base line.

The 103rd pitch Barker threw hit Whitt's bat and started for center field. This is when Manning began his jump for joy.

"I would have run all the way to the pitcher's mound to catch that one," said Manning. "There is no way I wasn't going to get that ball."

Manning didn't have to run anywhere. He just stood, arms upward for what seemed like minutes. The ball finally came down into his outstretched glove.

Leonard Harold Baker was perfect.

Barker, who led the Indians with 19 victories last year and is now 34-25 in a major league career that started in 1976 with Texas, was dazed afterwards.

Between chugs on a bottle of Gambrina Asti Spumante, he said, "I've never before concentrated like I did over those final three innings.

"The feeling I had is something I can't explain. I've never before experienced anything like it. I was so nervous near the end, I dropped the ball one time on the mound. My stomach was a wreck."

Barker was asked if there's anything left for him to accomplish after a perfect game.

"Sure," he said, "Strike out all 27 batters."

Don't put it past him.

Don Rogers

# Don Rogers—So Full of Life

## by BILL LIVINGSTON
### 6/86

A very wise man once said that, through suffering, drop by drop, we acquire understanding.

Sports' cup runs over with sorrow today, and whatever wisdom can be gleaned from Don Rogers' death seems far away. We have had enough of athletes dying young in this town—the Browns' Rogers, Cleveland States's Paul Stewart. Had the Cavaliers drafted Len Bias, as they almost did, it would have been a triple cross to bear. As it is, the weight seems insupportable enough.

In the public record, not a spot of blame fell to Stewart. He had a 60-year-old man's heart, and only the most sophisticated tests could have detected the problem.

Bias' death June 19 was caused, an autopsy showed, by cocaine. He was just beginning a career with the world's best basketball team, the Boston Celtics. Larry Bird, his prospective teammate, called it "the cruelest thing ever." If there was a meaning, it was that no one, not even an athlete in splendid condition, is invulnerable.

"Let's 'really' party," an acquaintance reportedly told Bias before the cocaine began its fatal rampage through his system.

Rogers liked to party, too. He played with a raging zest that spilled over the confines of the field.

The Browns' starting free safety, Rogers was a member of the "Dogs," the swaggering, taunting, heavy hitters who prowled the secondary. The Dogs even made up a poster last season, all of them decked out in tuxedos, pure-bred canines straining at the leashes they held in their hands. Life was tempting meat, and they were going to "sic" it.

Maybe Rogers, who was supposed to be married yesterday, went out of control at his Thursday night bachelor party. But

111

Paul Warfield of the Browns' staff said Rogers sounded normal just two hours before he was rushed to a hospital, his body in rebellion against whatever had happened to it.  It is difficult to believe a man strung out, beyond control, could manage such a conversation.

Still, there is mounting evidence that drugs were involved.  Dr. Joseph Pawlowski, the pathologist who conducted the autopsy in California, was quoted yesterday by the Associated Press as saying Rogers probably died of a drug overdose.  The question, obviously, is what happened in the two hours between Warfield's conversation with him and the arrival of emergency medical personnel.  It is into this gap that Rogers might have cast his life.  It is an almost unbelievably foolish thing to have done, in the wake of the Bias case.

If a drug overdose was the cause of death, you must wonder how many stilled hearts and empty lungs, how many bereaved families and how many fiancees denied the chance to be wives must there be before someone cries, "Enough"?

This much seems clear.  If there is a gap in professional sports' drug detection system, close it.

Athletes today have the time and the money to participate in this terrible sub-culture.  Many of them don't belong on a pedestal.  If fans insist on putting them on one, strap them to it with scrupulous testing for drugs and severe penalties for drug abuse.

It could only clear the great majority of the innocent.  And it conceivably might help someone whose cry for help was lost in a Dog's howl.

As far as a prospective drug policy goes, Browns' President Art Modell, sounding older and wearier than the 61 years of age he turned last week, yesterday called for immediate, random, mandatory testing throughout the league.  He said that he had asked for that many times and that his call was not linked to the events in Sacramento, California.

"Would you be surprised if drugs were involved (in Rogers' death)?" he was asked.

Modell sighed. He has been through too many of these too-sudden deaths since he became the man in charge of the Browns. (Ernie Davis, Don Fleming and Tom Bloom died in 1963.)

"Nothing surprises me anymore in football," Modell said.

If Rogers did die from drugs, a rush to judge him by the guardians of the public morals would surprise few. The public revulsion about drugs in sports has grown with each revelation of each death. If the Browns, with their enlightened "Inner Circle" drug-counselling program, could not reach Rogers, so the reasoning would go, then the hell with him.

But where does it say that your lasting memory of a man must be determined by the last impression he left?

Those who knew him on the Browns will remember him as a fine player, on a team that was on the rise.

From the press box, reporters remember him as a man who was seemingly involved in every big play that scorching January afternoon in Miami against the Dolphins in the playoffs. All of his plays weren't good ones, as he was once knocked over on a goal-line stand and once ran into a teammate on what could have been a touchdown interception return.

He had a few bad moments, many more good ones, and what struck you most of all was his eagerness to seize them as they came along and wring them dry.

Rogers was full of life, even in a violent game in which a career can end on the next snap of the ball. He poured himself into the game. That is why those who knew him have tears left to cry. That is why people hurt in this town this morning.

Don Rogers seemed to have wasted his life. And no matter how many times you go with this age-old flow of pain, it never gets any easier.

Bernie Kosar

# Browns Rally to Defeat Jets in

# Two Overtimes

### by TONY GROSSI
### 1/87

The best and the worst moments in Browns history unfolded in one exhilarating afternoon of football at the Stadium yesterday.

More than four hours after the game started Cleveland had its first playoff victory in 18 years.

Down by 10 points to the New York Jets with 4:14 to go, the Browns rallied to tie at 20-20 with seven seconds left in regulation.

Then they overcame a missed field goal by Mark Moseley from 23 yards in the first overtime before the veteran kicker atoned with the game-winner from 27 yards 2:02 into a second extra period.

When the third-longest game in National Football League history had ended, the Browns emerged 23-20 victors over the gasping Jets, keeping their unforgettable season alive with record-setting performances on offense and defense.

The Browns, 13-4 after their sixth victory, will play host in the AFC Championship Game next Sunday to the winner of today's Denver-New England playoff semifinal. That is the last stop before the Super Bowl.

"I played nine years to get here," said tight end Ozzie Newsome, who hauled in six catches for 114 yards. "We will be ready."

"I think we all had an opportunity to experience one of the finest games in the history of this sport," effused coach Marty Schottenheimer. "I have never experienced or seen a comeback like that."

The furious rally was led by quarterback Bernie Kosar, who set playoff records with 33 completions in 64 attempts for 489 yards. Two uncharacteristic interceptions by Kosar in the fourth quarter set the stage for the climax.

With the Jets holding a 13-10 lead in the fourth quarter, Kosar, frustrated in the middle periods, finally moved the Browns to the Jets' two. But on third down, the 23-year-old passer forced a ball to Webster Slaughter, who was double-covered. New York defensive back Russell Carter stole the pass in the corner of the end zone.

At that point, who didn't recall the fateful Brian Sipe interception that ended the 1980 season? Today marks the sixth anniversary of that dark day in Cleveland sports history.

After the Browns' defense forced the Jets to punt, Kosar took over at the Cleveland 17. Incredibly, his first pass, intended for Herman Fontenot, was intercepted by Jerry Holmes. Kosar had not thrown an interception since November and never had tossed two on successive passes.

Many fans in the crowd of 78,106 fled to the exits, cursing another letdown.

Before the non-believers had made it out, Jets running back Freeman McNeil bounced off the middle of the Browns' defensive pile, and raced around the right corner for a 25-yard touchdown. It gave the Jets their 20-10 lead.

Kosar and the Browns took the field with 4:08 to play.

"Bernie comes into the huddle and says, 'We're going to take this game,' said left tackle Paul Farren. "It's incredible the way he brought us together as a unit, one play at a time."

"The play that started it all was an inexcusable roughing-the-passer penalty on Jets' defensive end Mark Gastineau, long after a Kosar incompletion. Gastineau's mistake in judgment gave the Browns a first down at their 33.

Five completions—two to Reggie Langhorne, two to Brian Brennan and one to Curtis Dickey—moved the Browns to the one at the two-minute warning.

Kevin Mack plunged over guard Dan Fike for the touchdown, and Moseley's extra point made it 20-17, and gave the Browns hope.

Moseley's onside kick was recovered by the Jets at the Browns' 45, but the relentless Cleveland defense moved them three yards back in three plays and forced another punt.

The Browns took over at their 33 with :51 left. A pass interference penalty led them to the Jets' 42. Kosar then lofted a pass to Slaughter, who picked it off the helmet of cornerback Carl Howard and fell to the five.

After an incompletion, Schottenheimer sent in Moseley. The 13-year veteran poked it through from 22 yards to send the game into overtime.

That's when the Cleveland defense, which sacked Jets' quarterbacks Pat Ryan and Ken O'Brien a playoff record-tying nine times, dug in.

"We just felt if we could keep getting the ball in Bernie's hands, we'd win," said end Carl (Big Daddy) Hairston, who had nine tackles and three sacks.

The Jets won the overtime coin toss, but O'Brien, who replaced injured starter Ryan in the first half, could muster nothing.

From the Cleveland 26, Kosar marched the Browns to the Jets' five, covering the last 35 yards on a pass to Langhorne against a rare New York blitz.

Moseley was sent in again with 8:53 left in the overtime. He missed the 23-yard attempt at the closed end, wide right.

"I barely hit it," Moseley recounted. "I was off balance, falling away."

The Jets were stopped on the next two possessions.

"This was the best our defense has ever played," Schottenheimer said. "They kept making the plays when they had to in the third down situations."

The winning drive began at the Browns' 31 after Dave Jennings' playoff record 14th punt of the game.

By then, the beleaguered Jets' defense was physically spent.

The Jets had no fuel in their tanks.

"I didn't think they'd ever wear down, but they finally did," said center Mike Baab, who played the entire game with a sprained left knee.

Mack, gaining strength as the game approached the four-hour mark, ran for four yards and a first down to the Browns' 41, then banged ahead for eight yards to midfield two plays later. From the Jets' 42, Brennan broke up an errant pass that was nearly intercepted by the Jets' Howard.

"That was the biggest play of the game," Kosar said.

Given another life, the Browns' offensive line finally took the game in their huge hands. Fontenot ran for seven yards. Then Mack, on three successive, bullish carries, gained 26 to take the Browns to the Jets' nine. The Browns gained 45 of their total 75 rushing yards on the last series of the game.

The Jets called time to make Moseley think about his last miss.

"It was probably the worst thing they could do," said Moseley, who had won five games in overtime over his distinguished career. "I'm a good concentrator."

Moseley hammered the game-winner through the uprights at the devilish, open end of the Stadium.

The fans, who had stood and roared the entire 17 minutes and two seconds of overtime, went berserk.

"Just before we said our prayer in the locker room, I told the players to listen," said Schottenheimer. "You could still hear the people cheering for us.

"This is a victory, a game, a moment all of us will remember the rest of our lives."

With a wink, Kosar whispered to a reporter, "Just another day at the office."

# The Drive

## by BOB DOLGAN
### 1/87

The Browns' loss to Denver yesterday has to be one of the most disappointing in Cleveland sports history.

After the wondrous public mania of the last few weeks, after all the Super Bowl expectations, it is hard to swallow the fact that the Browns came apart in the final minutes after they appeared to have the game won.

The Browns had stopped Denver and quarterback John Elway all day. They had the Broncos pinned back on their own two-yard line with 5:32 to go. With a seven-point lead, you could smell Pasadena in the snowy air. The Super Bowl tickets were all but printed.

The impotent Denver offense had scored only 13 points, 10 of them after Cleveland errors. Since early in the second quarter, Denver had put only three points on the board.

But suddenly, the Broncos and Elway came out of the grave, tying the game with 37 seconds left in regulation and then winning in overtime.

What happened? Why did the Browns defenders go from heroes to bums?

Some Browns felt the coaches made a mistake in rushing Elway with three men instead of four during the tying and winning drives.

"When you get a quarterback like Elway, who can scramble, three guys are not going to be able to rush him," Browns safety Chris Rockins said. "It hurt us. Every time I looked back, he was running somewhere.

"I'm pretty sure we would have stopped them if we had rushed four men.

"We rushed with four men most of the game. That's what happens when you go away from the game plan. When

Brian Brennan spins around Dennis Smith for a 48-yard TD reception and an apparent Super Bowl berth.

they're 98 yards away, you should stop them. Now it makes me feel like everything went for naught."

End Sam Clancy said the same thing. "We were going with a three-man line," he said. "I don't think we got the pressure on Elway we should have. I would have liked to use a four-man line.

"Every time we used it during the game we popped Elway."

Coach Marty Schottenheimer has often stated that he prefers using the dime defense to prevent the long gain in such situations.

The only thing that it prevented yesterday was a trip to the Super Bowl.

Schottenheimer made another strange call when the Browns had the ball in overtime with a chance to win. On third down and two from the Cleveland 38, he tried a run for the first down. It failed. Why didn't he have quarterback Bernie Kosar pass? Kosar is his clutch man. He had just thrown a 48-yard TD pass to Brian Brennan for what looked like the winning score a few minuted earlier.

Now most of Cleveland is in mourning. This will be the gloomiest wake since the Browns lost the infamous playoff game to Oakland six years ago.

Defensive end Carl (Big Daddy) Hairston, who once played in a losing cause in a Super Bowl while in Philadelphia, said it was more disappointing to lose this game.

"This is the lowest I've felt since I can remember," said nose tackle Bob Golic, near tears.

"It's tough to get to the Super Bowl, especially when you know you don't have that many chances left," said the nine-year veteran linebacker Clay Matthews.

"It's a shocking feeling, the worst of my career," said Eddie Johnson. "Anytime you have a team on their two-yard line, and your defense is playing as well as we were, you shouldn't lose."

"I thought we had them when it was third-and-18," said Clancy, referring to a play from the Cleveland 48 during the tying drive, "but Elway drilled a pass right on the money. It feels terrible to lose a game like that, but it's the same way we won last week. All we can do now is look forward to next year."

During the winning Denver drive in overtime, Clancy just missed intercepting an Elway screen pass over his head. "If I had taken another step backwards, I think I would have had it," said Clancy.

On the next play, Elway threw a 28-yarder to Steve Watson to the 22, dooming the Browns. "We were in zone coverage," said Browns defensive back Felix Wright. "If I hadn't slipped on the play, I would have got to the ball. We have no excuses. We weren't tired. We were excited. We never thought they'd go 98 yards to tie it."

The Broncos got a gift TD when the Browns had only 10 men on the field on fourth down from the one-yard line in the second quarter. Veteran linebacker Brad Van Pelt made the mistake on that one.

According to several players, Van Pelt was on the field with the goal-line stand unit on the previous down. Eddie Johnson was hurt on the play and Mike Johnson ran in to replace him. Van Pelt assumed Denver was going to kick a field goal and that Mike Johnson was coming in to replace him. Van Pelt left the field.

Denver's Gerald Willhite then ran, barely scoring as Rockins tackled him at the goal line. "If Brad had been in there, we probably would have stopped it," said Rockins.

So now it's over. Too bad. But let's thank the Browns. They gave the city its most joyful ride on the whirlwind since the 1948 Indians. Wait until next year.

# The Fumble

## by DOUG CLARKE
### 1/88

It was The Mourning After—the day we were supposed to be all numb and drained and bitter and hung over from The Fumble that wagged the Dawgs' incredible comeback at Mile High Stadium—and the two black men were busy unloading crates from a truck in the alley of E. 4th Street outside of Otto Moser's restaurant.

There were a few pedestrians about, a bag lady with plenty of yesterdays in her cart, a man with a rheumy eye that held few tomorrows, a couple of men carrying briefcases, and myself. Suddenly, one of the men from the truck broke into song right there in the loading zone. He sang it with a box on his shoulder and a twinkle in his eye. He carried the tune well and it seemed to reverberate off the store fronts there in the narrow street.

"Bernie, Bernie . . . how you can throw . . . ." he sang.

The man's partner quickly picked up the tune and carried it the final two yards—the yards Earnest Byner traveled without the ball in those waning, agonizing moments Sunday at Mile High—going, "Oh, yeah . . . Bernie, Bernie . . . Su-per Bowl . . . "

The bag lady and the poor soul with the rheumy eye seemed not to notice, but the rest of us did and our eyes met, exchanging knowing looks. We shrugged together, perhaps a bit sheepishly, helping each other to smile. And then, in the early hours of the morning after we had lost to Denver . . . again . . . we were all chuckling together.

So don't worry about us, babe. Everything is okay here in Brownstown. We'll be totin' that barge, liftin' our bale just like always—hummin' and singin' even as our cheeks carry the grimy tracks of our tears. We roll with the punches, we do—even the most savage of them—and will live to woof

123

Earnest Byner lays on the goal line after fumbling late in the AFC
Championship game in Denver.

again another day. Count on it.

We are, after all, survivors. We survived the holocaust of The Lean Years, the shock of Red Right 88 (The Pass that wound up in the hands of the Raiders' Mike Davis), we survived the numbing totality of The Drive of last season and we'll survive The Fumble—Byner's boo-boo that came at the trail end of a play called Trap 13.

Say it ain't so? Hell, yes, it's so. And we'll wear it well, too, this bitter, seamy business of always coming up short. There is, to be sure, a certain poignancy to being a Browns fan now. Like being a Red Sox rooter. Or a Dodger fan from Flatbush in the 40's and 50's. Wait'll next year, dem Bums of Flatbush cried.

And so it is with us. What the hell. We'll be stronger for it. And, more importantly, so will the Cleveland Browns.

Did you notice the way Brian Brennan made a point of coming over and consoling Byner immediately after The Fumble? Did that first, "then" banged his fist against his helmet in frustration.

And did you see Bernie Kosar make what amounted to a death march—walking in front of the bench where his offensive line sat in a stupor, talking to them, taking care of business while giving Byner his moment alone? Did that first, "then" came around to Byner's side and put his arm around the shoulders that were the reason the Browns had scratched their way back into the game.

But the pure, crystalline moment that burns forever in our fevered mind is the one which captures Kosar's exit from the field—his head held high, before disappearing down the tunnel of broken dreams beneath the stands. Kosar looked . . . well, "majestic." His whole posture seemed to be addressing John Elway, his nemesis, saying, "Okay, Big Guy, you won again. You shot us down in another duel . . . But there'll be another day . . . another showdown . . . and I'm going to be the guy standing at he other end of the alley waiting for you . . . . "

You could almost see yet another indelible layer of character forming around Kosar's trusty, husky shoulders—hard and durable as steel milled in a Youngstown plant—irrevocably placed for the ages to marvel at.

What the hell. They "all" came off the field that way. Majestically. Even Byner. Maybe Byner most especially. A bunch of Charles Bronsons with faces ravaged by old sins and the scars of hurt and loss. Mr. Majestyk goes looking for the guy with the death wish, this Elway guy keeps on killing us. Stone cold, baby.

Right then and there you figured . . . no, "knew" . . . that there would be a next year. And a year after that. The duel going on and on . . . the Browns and the Broncos . . . Elway and Kosar . . . Kosar and Elway . . . until the villain, this Elway guy, gets his.

Damn, but this guy "is" good. You have to give him that. He just keeps coming at you with that bazooka he calls an arm, the long-toothed, grimace-smile behind the mask seeming to say to us, "It just keeps getting worse and worse, doesn't it?"

Fuck *you*, Elway. And the surfboard you rode into Denver on.

And yet, there was Bernie, The Nonchalant One, right there with him, staying on Elway's shoulders—a shadow and a legacy for the ages. Bobby Layne vs. Otto Graham . . . Kosar vs. Elway.

And to think we almost didn't get to feel "this" good. Face it: at halftime we were angry, bitter and disillusioned. And plenty pissed off, too—throwing Schottenheimer's words about how happy he was over the team's "preparation" back in his face. After all the buildup—the emotional high, the dawg bones and the "Bernie, Bernie" songs—this is what you guys come up with?

I remember sitting at the bar at Nighttown on Monday night of last week when a strange feeling came over me. I hadn't been able to get into this NFL season at all because of The Strike, scarcely noting and remembering little of the Browns ups and downs, and yet, now that the Denver game was coming up . . . the day of redemption for The Drive finally at hand . . . I got the overwhelming urge to tell the bartender to turn on the TV set. There was no TV in the bar at Nighttown, and yet I felt there "should" be one at that moment and that it was time for the Browns to play Denver. Never mind that the Browns had beaten the Colts just two days before. It was TIME. Time to get it on. I wanted to know the outcome right then and there.

Part of that feeling, I knew, was the knowledge that we would be inundated with football to the point of nausea in the pages of the *Plain Dealer* all week. And not just on the sports pages, either. All over the paper. Bullshit stuff. Features and crap and stats. Statistics no one reads because football is an emotional high, not a statistical one. NFL fluff stories. Editors ordering writers to write Browns-related stories, creating more space for advertising. By Saturday, I would be already tired of the game and they hadn't even played a damn thing yet.

". . . and this is what you guys come up with?"

I will not try to tell you I suspected all along that the Browns had such . . . someone used the word "courage," and that seems to nail down the essence of the club as well as anything . . . because it would not be true. Indeed, The Anatomy of a Notebook, my own, read like this at halftime:

"Browns losing ugly . . . also losing poise and composure (holding and roughing penalties etc.) . . . Sins of past rearing up to haunt: No pass rush, no blue-chip burner to make the big catch, no defense in Big Game (Dawgs turn to Puppies in the clutch) . . . maybe no guts when chips are down, either . . . Fans who went to Denver should send Modell a bill for the air fare and call it even . . . Injuries to Baab and Puzzuoli hurt. Ditty The Lindy (Infante) Waltz. Time to turn the game over to Bernie and let him wing it . . . "

So I sold 'em short. Maybe a lot of us did. Funny how one rotten half tends to obliterate recent successes as well as the senses. All the phobias and cynicism come galloping out of our closets. A legacy of the Modell Age, no doubt. That, too, makes us tougher in the long run.

In the end, I wouldn't have changed anything. Not even the outcome. "Especially" the outcome. We'll take our trip to the Super Bowl without an asterisk or a taint, thank you. The Byner fumble? Keep that on the record, too. Better Earnest with the stoic face than someone less heroic, someone less "deserving" of that fumble (say, a Herman Fontenot or a Clarence Weathers). Byner "earned" the right to that fumble. There was something very Cleveland-like in the way Byner, knowing he already had the first down, strove to make it in the end zone . . . to put us over the hump, as it were, just to get us even. It wasn't the time to Franco Harris-it. It was get down and dirty time. But the ball was jarred loose and the game came away with it.

No, the only thing that needed to be changed (score one for the notebook) was the Dawgs. Granted, they faced a villain from another planet in Elway, but if memory serves, the Dawgs have had other days against other top guns when they turned to puppies. Their tackling, especially, was atrocious. Indeed, the tackling in the secondary turned not one but two ordinary Elway completions into touchdowns. Erase those atrocities and maybe Byner is lunging for the score which would have put the game out of Elway's reach.

All of which leaves us exactly where today? At the end of a very long emotional rope of a season best forgotten and a title game that will be remembered for yet another year, one imagines. Disappointed, yes; bitter and angry, no. How do you get mad at a team that refused to quit and provide us with one of the most thrilling of championship games in the history of the NFL?

Reactions around town? Well, there was the man who said that the "only good thing about the game was that Art Modell didn't get to win a championship." There will always be that segment of the populace, of course, and a rejoinder to the effect that Modell is still one up on Gene Mauch would have fallen on deaf ears.

There was also the chalk blackboard in front of T. J. Ruggs' restaurant in the Arcade. The chalk-writing had once said, "Go Browns," but someone had erased the 'G' so that on Tuesday it said "O Browns."

In the cold light of day coming through the skylight above, the zip figure, as in coming up empty, spoke the truth and yet it seemed an awfully harsh judgment, all things considered.

By the time you read this . . . well, by next week at the very latest . . . we'll have pretty much digested this business of coming up short. Maybe we'll bump into someone who will say, "You know, I've just about reached the point where I've gotten over losing that game." And when the Super Bowl ends, a game we will mostly ignore, we will hear someone say, "Hey, I just realized . . . in another three weeks or so the pitchers and catchers report for spring training."

When this happens, we'll be back on even keel again. Maybe we're already there. Hell, we've been around "this" block before.

# AFTERWORD

Since 1946, in the forty-five year existence of the Cleveland Browns, the team has participated in postseason contests in twenty-five of those years. The Browns won the All-America Football Conference Championship four consecutive years, 1946-1949. They have captured the National Football League Championship on four occasions, 1950, 1954, 1955, and 1964.

The following Browns, who spent a significant or full part of their careers in Cleveland, are members of the Pro Football Hall of Fame: Jim Brown, Paul Brown, Len Ford, Frank Gatski, Otto Graham, Lou Groza, Dante Lavelli, Mike McCormack, Bobby Mitchell, Marion Motley, Paul Warfield, and Bill Willis.

The Cleveland Indians, since 1945, have brought home two American League pennants, in 1948 and 1954. The Tribe defeated the Boston Braves in 1948 to become world champions.

Here is the list of Cleveland ballplayers, playing many or all of their years in this city, who reside in Cooperstown: Earl Averill, Lou Boudreau, Jesse Burkett, Stan Coveleski, Bob Feller, Elmer Flick, Addie Joss, Nap Lajoie, Satchel Paige, Gaylord Perry, Joe Sewell, Tris Speaker, Early Wynn, and Cy Young. Al Lopez is in the Hall of Fame as a manager, and Bill Veeck as an owner.

Cleveland's Cavaliers, beginning with their inception in 1970, have been invited to postseason action seven times.

Nate Thurmond and Lenny Wilkins are enshrined in the Basketball Hall of Fame.

Between 1945 and 1973 (when they ceased operations) the Barons of the American Hockey League won seven Calder Cups, in 1944-45, 1947-48, 1950-51, 1952-53, 1953-54, 1956-57, and 1963-64.

# PERMISSIONS

Grateful acknowledgment is made to the following for permission to reprint previously published material:

Virginia Bradner: For "Baseball's World Champions" from *The Cleveland Indians* by Franklin Lewis. Originally published by Putnam's in 1949.

*The Call and Post*: For "Doby and Paige Help Tribe Win Pennant" by A. S. "Doc" Young. Original printing, 10/9/48.

Doug Clarke: For "The Fumble" from the *Cleveland Edition*. Previously published on 1/21/88.

*The Cleveland Press* Collection/Cleveland State University Archives: For "Browns Smash Colts for NFL Championship" by Bob August, 12/28/64; "Wounded Veteran Wins U. S. Open in Second Playoff Round" by Jack Clowser, 6/17/46; "A Hero is Traded, Colavito for Kuenn" by Frank Gibbons, 4/18/60; "Barker's Perfect Game" by Burt Graeff, 5/16/81; "Ernie Davis, A Dream Unfulfilled" by Bill Scholl, 5/18/63; "The Kardiac Kids" by Bob Sudyk, 12/22/80. All articles previously published in the *Cleveland Press*.

Rocky Colavito: For "Rocky Smacks Four Homers in One Game" from *Don't Knock the Rock* by Gordon Cobbledick. Copyright © 1966 by The World Publishing Company, Cleveland.

Kensington Publishing: For "Reflections on the Browns" from *Out of Bounds* by Jim Brown and Steve Delsohn. Published in 1989 by Zebra Books.

Bill Levy: For "Red Right 88" from *Sam, Sipe, and*

133

*Company: The Story of the Cleveland Browns* by Bill Levy. Published by J. T. & P. D. Dole, 1981.

*The Plain Dealer*: For "The Bad Old Days, Early Cavs" by Dan Coughlin, 4/27/76; "Rams Edge 'Skins in Bitter Cold" by John Dietrich; "The Drive" by Bob Dolgan, 1/12/87; "Graham's Swan Song, Another Title" by James E. Doyle, 12/26/55; "Browns Rally to Defeat Jets in Two Overtimes" by Tony Grossi, 1/4/87; "Score Hit in Eye" by Chuck Heaton, 5/857; "Giants Sweep Indians" by Harry Jones, 10/3/54; "Miracle in Richfield" by Hal Lebovitz, 4/30/76; "Don Rogers—So Full of Life" by Bill Livingston, 6/29/86; "Nicklaus Wins PGA and Record 14th Major" by Bill Nichols, 8/13/73; "Barons Win Calder Cup" by Thomas Place, 4/26/64; "Browns Rout Eagles in Their First NFL Contest" by Harold Sauerbrei.

The Putnam Berkley Group: For "Frank Robinson's Amazing Managerial Debut" from *Frank Robinson: The Making of a Manager* by Russell Schneider. Originally published by Coward, McCann & Geohegan, Inc. Copyright © 1976.

Sammis Publishing: For "The Greatest Football Game, Browns Vs. Rams" from *Pro Football's Great Moments* by Jack Clary. Copyright © 1983.

Sterling Lord Literistic Agency: For "Veeck on Doby" from *Veeck—As in Wreck* by Bill Veeck and Ed Linn. Published previously by Bantam in 1962.

# PHOTO CREDITS

135

# THE EDITOR

Mark Hodermarsky, a native Clevelander, teaches English at St. Ignatius High School in Cleveland, where he offers a course, *Baseball Literature*. His master's thesis, *Roger Angell and Baseball Prose: A Stylistic Analysis*, is in the National Baseball Library in Cooperstown. He resides in Olmsted Falls with his wife, Lynda, and children, Paul and Janet.